TRUSTING
JESUS

TRUSTING
JESUS

JEFFREY R. HOLLAND

**DESERET
BOOK**

SALT LAKE CITY, UTAH

Library of Congress Cataloging-in-Publication Data

Holland, Jeffrey R., 1940-
  Trusting Jesus / Jeffrey R. Holland.
      p.   cm.
  Includes index.
  ISBN 1-59038-155-6
  1. Jesus Christ—Mormon interpretations.   2. Christian life—Mormon authors.
  3. Church of Jesus Christ of Latter-day Saints—Doctrines.   I.Title.
  BX8643.J4H66   2003
  252'.09332—dc21   2003000083

Printed in the United States of America   18961
R. R. Donnelley and Sons, Crawfordsville, IN

10   9   8   7   6   5   4

Dedicated to all who seek hope

CONTENTS

INTRODUCTION

The title for this book and its first chapter was given to me by a neighbor, a four-year-old girl. The title for the last chapter was given to the whole world by the Apostle Paul, a missionary. A child and a missionary—two representative figures within the larger human family—who both know we must "trust Jesus." Each of the other chapters contributes testimonies from a variety of sources encouraging faith in the Savior of the world, love for His divine Father, and gratitude for the work of the Holy Spirit in communicating Their strength, comfort, and counsel to us.

Jesus once said to His very earliest followers, "What seek ye?" Whatever their answer—and ours—to that question, His response will always be the same: "Come," he says to each of us, "Come . . . follow me" (see John 1:38–43). That gentle invitation to trust the Savior's bidding and follow His ordained path is His constant declaration, whatever our individual quests and concerns. A fundamental truth decreed from before the foundation of earth is that His is the way of peace in this world and eternal life in the world to come. It is *the* Way, *the* Truth, and *the* Life.

Everyone meets affliction in mortality. Everyone knows some sorrow. Everyone experiences disappointments, even despair, and looks for ways to bear up and keep on going. The answer for all times and all seasons is to "trust Jesus." Through faith in Christ we will, like Alma, be "supported under trials and troubles of every kind" (Alma 36:27). I testify that I have been, and I have seen the promise fulfilled that the Savior is truly the "high priest of good things to come" (Heb. 9:11). My prayer for each reader is that you will feel that same security and safety always. In preparing this book I have wanted you to trust that Jesus "fainteth not, neither is weary. . . . He giveth power to the faint; and to them that have no might he increaseth strength. . . . They that wait upon the Lord shall renew their strength; they shall mount up with wings as eagles; they shall run, and not be weary; and they shall walk, and not faint" (Isa. 40:28–29, 31).

As always, I alone am responsible for the ideas and teachings contained in this collection. It is not an official publication of The Council of the First Presidency and Quorum of the Twelve Apostles nor a statement of official doctrines of The Church of Jesus Christ of Latter-day Saints. I wish to thank my able and supportive secretary, Randi Greene, and my friends at Deseret Book, especially Sheri Dew, Cory Maxwell, Jay Parry, and Tom Hewitson, for their unfailing (and in this case, long-distance) contribution to this effort. A special form of thanks always goes to my beloved wife, Pat, who not only encouraged the publication of this book but in every case has had to endure the anguish and travail her husband goes through when he prepares a message for delivery or an article for publication. I am eternally grateful to her and to the perfect children, children-in-law, and grandchildren God has given us.

As I leave the book in your hands, consider this from the Old Testament source which Christ referred to more often than any other: "The Lord is nigh unto them that are of a broken heart; and saveth such as be of a contrite spirit. Many are the afflictions of the righteous: but the Lord delivereth him out of them all. . . . The Lord redeemeth the soul of his servants: and none of them that trust in him shall be desolate" (Psalm 34:18–19, 22).

JRH
Santiago, 2003

I Am the Living Bread

1

TRUSTING JESUS

L ife in every era has had its troubles. Surely the Dark Ages were appropriately named, and not one of us is anxious to be transported back even to those later years of, say, the Hundred Years' War or the Black Plague. No, we're quite happy to have been born in a century of unprecedented material blessings and abundant living; yet in community after community, in small nations and large, we see individuals and families facing heightened anxiety and fear. It would seem that discouragement, depression, and despair are our contemporary "Black Plague." Ours is, as Jesus said it would be, a time of distress with perplexity (see Luke 21:25).

We know that some of the world's most painful suffering is done in silence, in the sorrow of a lonely life. But some of it has more violent expression. Millions around the world are, as one observer put it, "angry, armed and dangerous." In too many cities, drive-by shootings are becoming as common as drive-through laundries, and too many youngsters are packing a gun to school the way they used to pack a lunch.

There is an increasing feeling that time is out of joint, that no one seems wise enough or strong enough to set it right. In many cases, governments are in office but not in power, community values and neighborhood pride are often superficial or nonexistent, and too frequently the home is an alarming failure.

Furthermore, many of the social and political medicines of our day regularly miss the mark, so those would-be physicians stand by the bedside of "feverish and delirious humanity—outwitted, discredited, dumbfounded . . . not knowing in which direction to seek deliverance."[1]

If I may be so bold, may I suggest "direction for deliverance"? In words of one syllable, we need to turn to God and trust in His Only Begotten Son. We need to reaffirm our faith, and we need to reassert our hope. Where necessary we need to repent, and certainly we need to pray. It is the absence of spiritual fidelity that has led us to moral disarray in the twilight of the twentieth century. We have sown the wind of religious skepticism, and we are reaping the whirlwind of existential despair.

Without our religious faith, without recognizing the reality and necessity of spiritual life, the world makes no sense, and a nonsense world is a place of horror. Only if the world has meaning at a spiritual level is it possible for human beings to keep going, to keep trying. As Hamlet so wisely implored, so should we: "Angels and ministers of grace defend us!"[2]

My testimony is of the angels and ministers of grace who will always defend us if, as the prophet Alma commanded us, we "take care of . . . sacred things," we "look to God and live" (Alma 37:47). More prayer and humility, more faith and forgiveness, more repentance and revelation and reinforcement

4

from heaven—these are where we seek remedy and deliverance for "feverish and delirious humanity."

I testify of God's limitless love for His children, of His unquenchable desire to help us heal our wounds, individually and collectively. He *is* our Father, and Wordsworth wrote more than he knew when he said we came to earth "trailing clouds of glory . . . from God, who is our home."[3] But in far too many cases, we find no modern belief in a Heavenly Father, and when there is a belief, it is too often an erroneous one. God is not dead, and He is not an absentee landlord. God is not uncaring, or capricious, or cantankerous. Above all, He is not some sort of divine referee trying to tag us off third base.

The first and great commandment on earth is for us to love God with all our heart, might, mind, and strength (see Matt. 22:37; D&C 59:5), because surely the first and great promise in heaven is that He will always love us that way.

So much of what so many think about God (if they think about Him at all) must make Him weep. In fact, we know it makes Him weep. Could there be a more tender scene than this exchange recorded by Moses?

"And it came to pass that the God of heaven looked upon the residue of the people, and he wept; . . .

"And Enoch said unto the Lord: How is it that thou canst weep, seeing thou art holy, and from all eternity to all eternity? . . . How is it thou canst weep?

"The Lord said unto Enoch: Behold these thy brethren; they are the workmanship of mine own hands, and I gave unto them their knowledge, . . . and . . . gave I unto man his agency;

"And unto [them] have I . . . given commandment, that they should love one another, and that they should choose me, their Father; but behold, they are without affection, and they hate their own blood.

". . . the whole heavens . . . weep over them . . . ; wherefore should not the heavens weep, seeing these [who] suffer?" (Moses 7:28–29, 31–33, 37).

Angels and ministers of grace to defend us? They are all about us, and their holy sovereign, the Father of us all, is divinely anxious to bless us this very moment. Mercy is His mission, and love is His only labor. John Donne said once: "We ask our daily bread, and God never says, 'You should have come yesterday.' . . . [No, he says,] 'Today if you will hear my voice, today I will hear yours.' . . . If thou hast been benighted till now, wintered and frozen, clouded and eclipsed, damp and benumbed, smothered and stupefied till now, God yet comes to thee, not as in the dawning of the day, . . . but as the sun at [full] noon, to banish all shadows."[4]

Alma taught that truth to his son Helaman, entreating him to put his trust in heaven. He said that God was "quick to hear the cries of his people and [quick] to answer their prayers" (Alma 9:26). Out of very personal experience, Alma testified, "I have been supported [in] trials and troubles [and afflictions] of every kind . . . ; God has delivered me . . . ; I do put my trust in him, and he will still deliver me" (Alma 36:27).

My witness is that He will deliver all the rest of us, too, that He will deliver the entire human family, if we will but "take care of sacred things." The greatest affirmation of that promise ever given in this world was the gift of God's perfect and precious Firstborn Son, a gift given not in condemnation of the world, but to soothe and save and make the world secure: "For God so loved the world, that he gave his only begotten Son, that whosoever believeth in him should *not* perish, but have everlasting life" (John 3:16; emphasis added). But as the scriptures lament, "What doth it profit a man if a gift is bestowed upon him and he receive not the gift?" (D&C 88:33). I pray we will receive and embrace this infinite and eternal offering, recognizing that in the Lord Jesus Christ is our only hope and our only salvation.

Katie Lewis is my neighbor. Her father, Randy, is my bishop; her mother, Melanie, is a saint. And her older brother, Jimmie, is battling leukemia.

Sister Lewis recently recounted for me the unspeakable fear and grief that came to their family when Jimmie's illness was diagnosed. She spoke of the tears and the waves of sorrow that any mother would experience with a prognosis as grim as Jimmie's was. But like the faithful Latter-day Saints they are, the Lewises turned to God with urgency and with faith and with hope. They fasted and prayed, prayed and fasted. And they went again and again to the temple.

One day Sister Lewis came home from a temple session weary and worried, feeling the impact of so many days—and nights—of fear being held at bay only by monumental faith.

As she entered her home, four-year-old Katie ran up to her with love in her eyes and a crumpled sheaf of papers in her hand. Holding the papers out to her mother, she said enthusiastically, "Mommy, do you know what these are?"

Sister Lewis said frankly her first impulse was to deflect Katie's zeal and say she didn't feel like playing just then. But she thought of her children—all her children—and the possible regret of missed opportunities and little lives that pass too swiftly. So she smiled through her sorrow and said, "No, Katie. I don't know what they are. Please tell me."

"They are the scriptures," Katie beamed back, "and do you know what they say?"

Sister Lewis stopped smiling, gazed deeply at this little child,

7

knelt down to her level, and said, "Tell me, Katie. What do the scriptures say?"

"They say, 'Trust Jesus.'" And then she was gone.

Sister Lewis said that as she stood back up, holding a fistful of her four-year-old's scribbling, she felt near-tangible arms of peace encircle her weary soul and a divine stillness calm her troubled heart.

Katie Lewis, "angel and minister of grace," I'm with you. In a world of some discouragement, sorrow, and overmuch sin, in times when fear and despair seem to prevail, when humanity is feverish with no worldly physicians in sight, I too say, "Trust Jesus." Let Him still the tempest and ride upon the storm. Believe that He can lift mankind from its bed of affliction, in time and in eternity.

> Oh, dearly, dearly has he loved!
> And we must love him too,
> And trust in his redeeming blood,
> And try his works to do.[5]

Notes

From a talk given at general conference, October 1993.

1. Charles Edward Jefferson, *The Character of Jesus* (Salt Lake City: Parliament Publishers, 1968), 17.

2. William Shakespeare, *Hamlet*, act 1, scene 4, line 39.

3. William Wordsworth, "Ode: Intimations of Immortality" in *Complete Poetical Works of William Wordsworth* (St. Martin's Street, London: Macmillan and Co., 1924), 359.

4. John Donne, *Complete Poetry and Selected Prose of John Donne and the Complete Poetry of William Blake* (New York: Random House, 1941), 364.

5. Cecil Frances Alexander, "There Is a Green Hill Far Away," in *Hymns of The Church of Jesus Christ of Latter-day Saints* (Salt Lake City: The Church of Jesus Christ of Latter-day Saints, 1985), no. 194.

2

"He Hath Filled the Hungry with Good Things"

S ome time ago, I read an essay referring to "metaphysical hunger" in the world. The author was suggesting that the souls of men and women were dying, so to speak, from lack of spiritual nourishment in our time. That phrase, "metaphysical hunger," came back to me last month when I read the many richly deserved tributes paid to Mother Teresa of Calcutta. One correspondent recalled her saying that as severe and wrenching as physical hunger was in our day—something she spent virtually her entire life trying to alleviate—nevertheless, she believed that the absence of spiritual strength, the paucity of spiritual nutrition, was an even more terrible hunger in the modern world.

These observations reminded me of the chilling prophecy from the prophet Amos, who said so long ago, "Behold, the days come, saith the Lord God, that I will send a famine in the land, not a famine of bread, nor a thirst for water, but of hearing the words of the Lord" (Amos 8:11).

As the world slouches into the twenty-first century, many long for something, sometimes cry out for something, but too often scarcely know for what. The economic condition in the world, speaking generally and certainly not specifically, is probably better than it has ever been in history, but the human heart is still anxious and often filled with great stress. We live in an "information age" that has a world of data available literally at our fingertips, yet the meaning of that information and the satisfaction of using knowledge in some moral context seems farther away for many than ever before.

The price for building on such sandy foundations is high. Too many lives are buckling when the storms come and the winds blow (see Matt. 7:24–27). In almost every direction, we see those who are dissatisfied with present luxuries because of a gnawing fear that others somewhere have more of them. In a world desperately in need of moral leadership, too often we see what Paul called "spiritual wickedness in high places" (Eph. 6:12). In an absolutely terrifying way, we see legions who say they are bored with their spouses, their children, and any sense of marital or parental responsibility toward them. Still others, roaring full speed down the dead-end road of hedonism,* shout that they will indeed live by bread alone, and the more of it the better. We have it on good word, indeed we have it from the Word Himself, that bread alone—even a lot of it—is not enough (see Matt. 4:4; John 1:1).

During the Savior's Galilean ministry, He chided those who had heard of Him feeding the 5,000 with only five barley loaves and two fishes and now flocked to Him expecting a free lunch.

* doctrine that pleasure is the principal good.

That food, important as it was, was incidental to the real nourishment He was trying to give them.

"Your fathers did eat manna in the wilderness, and are dead," He admonished them. "I am the living bread which came down from heaven: if any man eat of this bread, he shall live for ever."

But this was not the meal they had come for, and the record says, "From that time many of his disciples went back, and walked no more with him" (John 6:49, 51, 66).

In that little story is something of the danger in our day. It is that in our contemporary success and sophistication we, too, may walk away from the vitally crucial bread of eternal life; we may actually *choose* to be spiritually malnourished, willfully indulging in a kind of spiritual anorexia. Like those childish Galileans of old, we may turn up our noses when divine sustenance is placed before us. Of course the tragedy then as now is that one day, as the Lord Himself has said, "In an hour when ye think not the summer shall be past, and the harvest ended," and we will find that our "souls [are] not saved" (D&C 45:2; see Jer. 8:20).

I have wondered if someone reading this might feel he or she or those they love are too caught up in the "thick of these thin things," are hungering for something more substantial and asking with the otherwise successful young man of the scriptures, "What lack I yet?" (Matt. 19:20). I have wondered if someone reading this might be wandering "from sea to sea," running "to and fro" as the prophet Amos said (Amos 8:12), wearied by the pace of life in the fast lane or in trying to keep up with the Joneses before the Joneses refinance. I have wondered if any have picked up this book hoping to find the answer to a deeply personal problem or to have some light cast on the most serious questions of their heart. Such problems or questions often deal with our marriages, our families, our friends, our health, our peace—or the conspicuous lack of such cherished possessions.

It is to those who so hunger that I address these thoughts. Wherever you live, and at whatever point in age or experience you find yourself, I declare that God has through His Only Begotten Son lifted the famine of which Amos spoke. I testify that the Lord Jesus Christ is the Bread of Life and a Well of Living Water springing up unto eternal life. I declare to those who are members of The Church of Jesus Christ of Latter-day Saints, and especially to those who are not, that our Heavenly Father and His Beloved Firstborn Son did appear to the boy prophet Joseph Smith and restored light and life, hope and direction, to a wandering world, a world filled with those who wonder, "Where is hope? Where is peace? What path should I follow? Which way should I go?"

Regardless of past paths taken or not taken, we wish to offer you "the way, the truth, and the life" (John 14:6). We invite you to join in the adventure of the earliest disciples of Christ who also yearned for the bread of life—those who did *not* go back but who came to Him, stayed with Him, and who recognized that for safety and salvation there was no other to whom they could ever go (see John 6:68).

You will recall that when Andrew and another disciple, probably John, first heard Christ speak, they were so moved and attracted to Jesus that they followed Him as He left the crowd. Sensing that He was being pursued, Christ turned and asked the two men, "What seek ye?" (John 1:38). Other translations render that simply "What do you want?" They answered, "Where dwellest thou?" or "Where do you live?" Christ said simply,

"Come and see" (John 1:38–39). Just a short time later, He formally called Peter and other new Apostles with the same spirit of invitation. To them He said, Come, "follow me" (Matt. 4:19).

It seems that the essence of our mortal journey and the answers to the most significant questions in life are distilled down to these two very brief elements in the opening scenes of the Savior's earthly ministry. One element is the question put to every one of us on this earth: "What seek ye? What do you want?" The second is His response to our answer, *whatever that answer is.* Whoever we are and whatever we reply, His response is *always* the same: "Come," He says lovingly. "Come, follow me." Wherever you are going, first come and see what I do, see where and how I spend my time. Learn of me, walk with me, talk with me, believe. Listen to me pray. In turn you will find answers to your own prayers. God will bring rest to your souls. Come, follow me.

With one voice and one accord, we bear witness that the gospel of Jesus Christ is the only way to satisfy ultimate spiritual hunger and slake definitive spiritual thirst. Only He who was so mortally wounded knows how to heal our modern wounds. Only One who was with God, and was God (see John 1:1), can answer the deepest and most urgent questions of our soul. Only His almighty arms could have thrown open the prison gates of death that otherwise would have held us in bondage forever. Only on His triumphant shoulders can we ride to celestial glory—if we will but choose through our faithfulness to do so.

To those who may feel they have somehow forfeited their place at the table of the Lord, we say again with the Prophet Joseph Smith that God has "a forgiving disposition," that Christ is "merciful and gracious, slow to anger, [is] long-suffering and full of goodness."[1] I have always loved that while Matthew records Jesus' great injunction, "Be ye therefore perfect, even as your Father which is in heaven is perfect" (Matt. 5:48), Luke adds the Savior's additional commentary: "Be ye therefore merciful, as your Father also is merciful" (Luke 6:36)—as if to suggest that mercy is at least a beginning synonym for the perfection God has and for which all of us must strive. Mercy, with its sister virtue forgiveness, is at the very heart of the Atonement of Jesus Christ and the eternal plan of salvation. Everything in the gospel teaches us that we can change if we need to, that we can be helped if we truly want it, that we can be made whole, whatever the problems of the past.

Now, if you feel too spiritually maimed to come to the feast, please realize that the Church is not a monastery for perfect people, though all of us ought to be striving on the road to godliness. No, at least one aspect of the Church is more like a hospital or an aid station, provided for those who are ill and want to get well, where one can get an infusion of spiritual nutrition and a supply of sustaining water in order to keep on climbing.

In spite of life's tribulations and as fearful as some of our prospects are, I testify that there is help for the journey. There is the Bread of Eternal Life and the Well of Living Water. Christ has overcome the world—our world—and His gift to us is peace now and exaltation in the world to come (see D&C 59:23). Our fundamental requirement is to have faith in Him and follow Him—always. I testify that in my fears and in my infirmities the Savior has surely sustained me. I will never be able to thank Him enough for such personal kindness and such loving care.

President George Q. Cannon said once: "No matter how serious the trial, how deep the distress, how great the affliction, [God] will never desert us. He never has, and He never will. He cannot do it. It is [against] His character [to do so]. He is an unchangeable being. . . . He will stand by us. We may pass through the fiery furnace; we may pass through deep waters; but we shall not be consumed nor overwhelmed. We shall emerge from all these trials and difficulties the better and the purer for them, if we only trust in our God and keep His commandments."[2]

Those who will receive the Lord Jesus Christ as the source of their salvation will always lie down in green pastures, no matter how barren and bleak the winter has been. And the waters of their refreshment will always be still waters, no matter how turbulent the storms of life. In walking His path of righteousness, our souls will be forever restored; and though that path may for us, as it did for Him, lead through the very valley of the shadow of death, yet we will fear no evil. The rod of His priesthood and the staff of His Spirit will always comfort us. And when we hunger and thirst in the effort, He will prepare a veritable feast before us, a table spread even in the presence of our enemies—contemporary enemies—which might include fear or family worries, sickness or personal sorrow of a hundred different kinds. In a crowning act of compassion at such a supper, He anoints our head with oil and administers a blessing of strength to our soul. Our cup runneth over with His kindness, and our tears runneth over with joy. We weep to know that such goodness and mercy shall follow us all the days of our life, and that we will, if we desire it, dwell in the house of the Lord forever (see Ps. 23).

I pray that all who are hungering and thirsting, and sometimes wandering, will hear this invitation from Him who is the Bread of Life, the Fountain of Living Water, the Good Shepherd of us all, the Son of God: "Come unto me, all ye that labour and are heavy laden, . . . and ye shall find rest unto your souls" (Matt. 11:28–29). Truly, He does fill "the hungry with good things," as His own mother, Mary, testified (Luke 1:53). Come, and feast at the table of the Lord in what I testify to be His true and living Church, led by a true and living prophet.

Notes

From a talk given at general conference, October 1997.

1. Joseph Smith, *Lectures on Faith* (Salt Lake City: Deseret Book, 1985), 42.
2. George Q. Cannon, "Freedom of the Saints," in *Collected Discourses*, comp. Brian H. Stuy, 5 vols. (Burbank, Calif., and Woodland Hills, Ut.: B. H. S. Publishing, 1987–92), 2:185.

3

"THIS DO IN
REMEMBRANCE OF ME"

T he hours that lay immediately ahead would change the meaning of all human history. It would be the crowning moment of eternity, the most miraculous of all the miracles. It would be the supreme contribution to a plan designed from before the foundation of the world for the happiness of every man, woman, and child who would ever live in it. The hour of atoning sacrifice had come. God's own Son, His Only Begotten Son in the flesh, was about to become the Savior of the world.

The setting was Jerusalem. The season was that of the Passover, a celebration rich in symbolism for what was about to come. Long ago the troubled and enslaved Israelites had been "passed over," spared, finally made free by the blood of a lamb sprinkled on the lintel and doorposts of their Egyptian homes (see Ex. 12:21–24). That, in turn, had been only a symbolic reiteration of what Adam and all succeeding prophets were taught from the beginning—that the pure and unblemished lambs offered from the firstlings of Israel's flocks were a similitude, a token, a prefiguration of the great and last sacrifice of Christ which was to come (see Moses 5:5–8).

Now, after all those years and all those prophecies and all those symbolic offerings, the type and shadow was to become reality. On this night when Jesus' mortal ministry was concluding, the declaration made by John the Baptist when that ministry had begun now meant more than ever—"Behold the Lamb of God" (John 1:29).

As a final and specially prepared Passover supper was ending, Jesus took bread, blessed and broke it, and gave it to His Apostles, saying, "Take, eat" (Matt. 26:26). "This is my body which is given for you: this do in remembrance of me" (Luke 22:19). In a similar manner, He took the cup of wine, traditionally diluted with water, said a blessing of thanks for it, and passed it to those gathered about Him, saying: "This cup is the new testament in my blood," "which is shed . . . for the remission of sins." "This do in remembrance of me." "For as often as ye eat this bread, and drink this cup, ye do shew the Lord's death till he come" (Luke 22:20; Matt. 26:28; Luke 22:19; 1 Cor. 11:26).

Since that upper room experience on the eve of Gethsemane and Golgotha, children of the promise have been under covenant to remember Christ's sacrifice in this newer, higher, more holy and personal way.

With a crust of bread, always broken, blessed, and offered first, we remember His bruised body and broken heart, His physical suffering on the cross where He cried, "I thirst," and finally, "My God, my God, why hast thou forsaken me?" (John 19:28; Matt. 27:46).

The Savior's physical suffering guarantees that through His mercy and grace every member of the human family shall be freed from the bonds of death and be resurrected triumphantly from the grave (see 2 Ne. 2:8). Of course, the time of that resurrection and the degree of glory it leads to are based upon our faithfulness.

With a small cup of water, we remember the shedding of Christ's blood and the depth of His spiritual suffering, anguish which began in the Garden of Gethsemane. There He said, "My soul is exceeding sorrowful, even unto death" (Matt. 26:38). He was in agony and "prayed more earnestly: and his sweat was as it were great drops of blood falling down to the ground" (Luke 22:44).

The Savior's spiritual suffering and the shedding of His innocent blood, so lovingly and freely given, paid the debt for what the scriptures call the "original guilt" of Adam's transgression (Moses 6:54). Furthermore, Christ suffered for the sins and sorrows and pains of all the rest of the human family, providing remission for all of our sins as well, upon conditions of obedience to the principles and ordinances of the gospel He taught (see 2 Ne. 9:21–23). As the Apostle Paul wrote, we were "bought with a price" (1 Cor. 6:20). What an expensive price and what a merciful purchase!

That is why every ordinance of the gospel focuses in one way or another on the Atonement of the Lord Jesus Christ, and surely that is why this particular ordinance with all its symbolism and imagery comes to us more readily and more repeatedly than any other in our lives. It comes in what has been called "the *most sacred,* the *most holy,* of all the meetings of the Church."[1]

Perhaps we do not always attach that kind of meaning to

our weekly sacramental service. How "sacred" and how "holy" is it? Do we see it as *our* passover, remembrance of *our* safety and deliverance and redemption?

With so very much at stake, this ordinance commemorating our escape from the angel of darkness should be taken more seriously than it sometimes is. It should be a powerful, reverent, reflective moment. It should encourage spiritual feelings and impressions. As such it should not be rushed. It is not something to "get over" so that the real purpose of a sacrament meeting can be pursued. This *is* the real purpose of the meeting. And everything that is said or sung or prayed in those services should be consistent with the grandeur of this sacred ordinance.

The administration and passing of the sacrament is preceded by a hymn which all of us should sing. It doesn't matter what kind of musical voice we have. Sacramental hymns are more like prayers anyway—and everyone can give voice to a prayer!

> *We may not know, we cannot tell,*
> *What pains he had to bear,*
> *But we believe it was for us*
> *He hung and suffered there.*[2]

It is an important element of our worship to unite in such lyrical and moving expressions of gratitude.

In that sacred setting, we ask you young men of the Aaronic Priesthood to prepare and bless and pass these emblems of the Savior's sacrifice worthily and reverently. What a stunning privilege and sacred trust given at such a remarkably young age! I can think of no higher compliment heaven could pay you. We do love you. Live your best and look your best when you participate in the sacrament of the Lord's Supper.

May I suggest that wherever possible a white shirt be worn by the deacons, teachers, and priests who handle the sacrament. For sacred ordinances in the Church we often use ceremonial clothing, and a white shirt could be seen as a gentle reminder of the white clothing you wore in the baptismal font and an anticipation of the white shirt you will soon wear into the temple and onto your missions.

That simple suggestion is not intended to be pharisaic or formalistic. We do not want deacons or priests in uniforms or unduly concerned about anything but the purity of their lives. But how our young people dress can teach a holy principle to us all, and it certainly can convey sanctity. As President David O. McKay taught, a white shirt contributes to the sacredness of the holy sacrament.[3]

In the simple and beautiful language of the sacramental prayers those young priests offer, the principal word we hear seems to be *remember.* In the first and slightly longer prayer offered over the bread, mention is made of a willingness to take upon us the name of the Son of God and to keep the commandments He has given us.

Neither of those phrases is repeated in the blessing on the water, though surely both are assumed and expected. What *is* stressed in both prayers is that all of this is done in remembrance of Christ. In so participating, we witness that we will always remember Him, that we may always have His Spirit to be with us (see D&C 20:77, 79).

If remembering is the principal task before us, what might come to our memories when those plain and precious emblems are offered to us?

We could remember the Savior's premortal life and all that we know Him to have done as the great Jehovah, creator of

21

heaven and earth and all things that in them are. We could remember that even in the grand council of heaven He loved us and was wonderfully strong, that we triumphed even there by the power of Christ and our faith in the blood of the Lamb (see Rev. 12:10–11).

We could remember the simple grandeur of His mortal birth to just a young woman, one probably in the age range of those in our Young Women organization, who spoke for every faithful woman in every dispensation of time when she said, "Behold the handmaid of the Lord; be it unto me according to thy word" (Luke 1:38).

We could remember His magnificent but virtually unknown foster father, a humble carpenter by trade who taught us, among other things, that quiet, plain, unpretentious people have moved this majestic work forward from the very beginning, and still do so today. If you are serving almost anonymously, please know that so, too, did one of the best men who has ever lived on this earth.

We could remember Christ's miracles and His teachings, His healings and His help. We could remember that He gave sight to the blind and hearing to the deaf and motion to the lame and the maimed and the withered. Then, on those days when we feel our progress has halted or our joys and views have grown dim, we can press forward steadfastly in Christ, with unshaken faith in Him and a perfect brightness of hope (see 2 Ne. 31:19–20).

We could remember that even with such a solemn mission given to Him, the Savior found delight in living; He enjoyed people and told His disciples to be of good cheer. He said we should be as thrilled with the gospel as one who had found a great treasure, a veritable pearl of great price, right on our own doorstep. We could remember that Jesus found special joy and happiness in children and said all of us should be more like them—guileless and pure, quick to laugh and to love and to forgive, slow to remember any offense.

We could remember that Christ called His disciples friends, and that friends are those who stand by us in times of loneliness or potential despair. We could remember a friend we need to contact or, better yet, a friend we need to make. In doing so we could remember that God often provides His blessings through the compassionate and timely response of another. For someone nearby we may be the means of heaven's answer to a very urgent prayer.

We could—and should—remember the wonderful things that have come to us in our lives and that "all things which are good cometh of Christ" (Moro. 7:24). Those of us who are so blessed could remember the courage of those around us who face more difficulty than we, but who remain cheerful, who do the best they can, and trust that the Bright and Morning Star will rise again for them—as surely He will do (see Rev. 22:16).

On some days we will have cause to remember the unkind treatment He received, the rejection He experienced, and the injustice—oh, the injustice—He endured. When we, too, then face some of that in life, we can remember that Christ was also "troubled on every side, [but] not distressed; . . . perplexed, but not in despair; persecuted, but not forsaken; cast down, but not destroyed" (2 Cor. 4:8–9).

When those difficult times come to us, we can remember that Jesus had to descend below all things before He could ascend above them, and that He suffered pains and afflictions and temptations of every kind that He might be filled with mercy and know how to succor His people in their infirmities (see Alma 7:11–12; D&C 88:6).

23

All this we could remember when we are invited by a kneeling young priest to remember Christ always.

We no longer include a supper with this ordinance, but it is a feast nevertheless. We can be fortified by it for whatever life requires of us, and in so doing we will be more compassionate to others along the way.

One request Christ made of His disciples on that night of deep anguish and grief was that they stand by Him, stay with Him in His hour of sorrow and pain. "Could ye not watch with me one hour?" He asked longingly (Matt. 26:40). I think He asks that again of us, every Sabbath day when the emblems of His life are broken and blessed and passed.

> How great the wisdom and the love
> That filled the courts on high
> And sent the Savior from above
> To suffer, bleed, and die![4]

"Oh, it is wonderful, wonderful to me!"[5] I bear witness of Him who is the Wonder of it all, even Jesus Christ.

Notes

From a talk given at general conference, October 1995.

1. Joseph Fielding Smith, *Doctrines of Salvation*, comp. Bruce R. McConkie, 3 vols. (Salt Lake City: Bookcraft, 1954–56), 2:340.

2. Cecil Frances Alexander, "There Is a Green Hill Far Away," in *Hymns of The Church of Jesus Christ of Latter-day Saints* (Salt Lake City: The Church of Jesus Christ of Latter-day Saints, 1985), no. 194.

3. See David O. McKay, Conference Report, October 1956, 89.

4. Eliza R. Snow, "How Great the Wisdom and the Love," in *Hymns*, no. 195.

5. Charles H. Gabriel, "I Stand All Amazed," in *Hymns*, no. 193.

4

TEACHING, PREACHING, HEALING

I would like to share some suggestions for teachers (and applications for all of us, including parents and teachers) as we teach of Christ. But first some general observations.

I suppose it's proverbial in every generation to quote Charles Dickens and mutter, "It was the best of times, it was the worst of times."[1] As a general observation, I think our youth are wonderful, that they're striving collectively to be as fine a generation of young people as we have ever had in this Church. But even as I say that, I am quick to acknowledge that exceptions to that rule are too many and often far too serious. When our youth sin now, they can do so in such flagrantly offensive ways with ever more serious consequences in their lives. That is the world we are in, and it is, by scriptural definition, a world that is getting progressively more wicked.

So over time we will continue to see a steady deterioration of what is acceptable in movies, on television, in pop music

25

(which, in the case of rap lyrics, isn't even music at all), and, perhaps in our most dangerous contemporary foe, abuse of the Internet. I have learned what you have learned—that the door to permissiveness, the door to promiscuity and lewdness, swings only one way. It only opens farther and farther; it never swings back. Individuals can choose to close it, but it is quite certain, historically speaking, that public appetite and public policy will never close it.

That is where you and the Church come in. Don't count on laws or legislatures or courts or civil authorities or anyone else to provide our defense. Our defense is a burning conviction of the gospel of Jesus Christ and a keeping of those commandments. Our defense is in prayer and faith, in study and fasting, in the gifts of the Spirit, the ministration of angels, the power of the priesthood. And, in some significant ways, our defense is you.

Now, what is your arsenal in this battle? With what will you conquer? When we stand in the role of teachers, it is primarily one thing. Your weapon is the holy word of God, the scriptures. In this fight, and it is a fight, we all come to stand with Alma eventually. We too realize sooner or later that "the preaching [or, in your case, the teaching] of the word had a great tendency to lead the people to do that which was just—yea, it had had more powerful effect upon the minds of the people than the sword, or anything else, which had happened unto them— therefore Alma thought it was expedient that they should try the virtue of the word of God" (Alma 31:5).

Over the years, you and I have taught Paul's marvelous injunction to "put on the whole armour of God" (Eph. 6:11), a commandment reiterated in our day in section 27 of the Doctrine and Covenants (see v. 15). In that description of preparing for spiritual battle, I have been impressed that most of the protection the Lord outlines for us there is somewhat defensive. The revelation speaks of breastplates and shields and helmets, all of which are important and protective but which leave us, in a sense, without an actual weapon yet. Are we only to be on the defensive? Are we simply to ward off blows and see it through and never be able, spiritually speaking, to strike a blow? No. We are supposed to advance in this and win a battle that started in heaven long ago. So we need some kind of even chance on the offense, and we are given it. You are given it. The weapon that is mentioned, the thing that allows us to actu-ally do battle with the "darkness of this world," to use Paul's phrase, is "the sword of the Spirit, which is *the word of God*" (Eph. 6:12, 17; emphasis added). May I repeat that? "The sword of the Spirit, which is the word of God." I love that marriage of spiritual concepts.

Coupled with prayer and the power of the priesthood that ought to be in all of our lives, I believe the greatest source of spirituality available to our youth (and everyone else) is the word of God, the scriptures, the revelations. Martin Luther and the Reformers were closer to the truth than they knew when they taught that the scriptures are a means of grace. They didn't have it entirely right, but they knew they were onto some-thing—that the scriptures had a great central role in the church of God, that hearing the word of God and, later, when they could, reading the word of God was a privilege every lay member of the church was to enjoy. Every man or woman or even child was to have a direct relationship with Deity through the study of the scriptures. That is a principle within the Refor-mation, which set the stage for scriptures in the Restoration.

It is little wonder that as times get tougher and the going

gets rockier, the Brethren have focused our curriculum at every level on the scriptures. Please immerse yourself in them and immerse your students in them. Don't stray off into forbidden paths and get lost in mists of darkness. You know what happened to those folks! Stay with the rod of iron, which is the word of God. Use what teaching techniques you need to assist with your lesson, but keep war stories and strange doctrines and near-death experiences to a minimum. Stay in the heart of the mine where the real gold is. And what gold there is in the New Testament!

Always try to give your students the "big picture." I know you have specific lessons to teach and that there is a terribly limited time in which to get those lessons completed. I know that. I've been with you. But even as I acknowledge that you can't teach everything, nevertheless I invite you to occasionally give your students the benefit of a broader view, a view that *isn't* going to be contained in any specific lesson or any given verse. Teach them how to read the scriptures with some sense of wholeness and perspective in mind.

Let me give you an example. We quickly and readily think of Christ as a teacher. I always have and always will. The greatest teacher who ever lived or ever will live. The New Testament is full of His teachings, His sayings, His sermons, His parables. One way or another He is a teacher on every page of that book. But even as He taught, He was consciously doing something in addition to that, something that put teaching in perspective.

After the account of His nativity and His childhood, about which we know relatively little, we are told of Christ's baptism at the hands of John. Then He is led up into the wilderness "to be with God," not the devil. "To be with God," the Joseph Smith Translation tells us (JST, Matt. 4:1).

Following the temptations that were presented by the adversary and the Savior's successful triumph over them, Christ makes His initial call to those first disciples (not yet Apostles), and the work begins.

This is what Matthew says:

"And Jesus went about all Galilee, *teaching* in their synagogues, and *preaching* the gospel of the kingdom, and *healing* all manner of sickness and all manner of disease among the people" (Matt. 4:23; emphasis added).

Now the teaching and the preaching we know and would expect. Furthermore, we know there were miracles of every kind, healings of many of the afflicted. But I remember the first time I realized that from this earliest beginning, from the first hour, healing is mentioned as if it were a synonym for teaching and preaching. In fact, the passage being cited goes on to say more about the healing than the teaching.

Matthew continues:

"And his fame went throughout all Syria: and they brought unto him all sick people that were taken with divers diseases and torments, and those which were possessed with devils, and those which were lunatick, and those that had the palsy; and he healed them" (Matt. 4:24).

What then follows is the masterful Sermon on the Mount, six and a half pages that would take six and a half years to teach properly, I suppose. But the moment that sermon is over, He comes down from the mountain and is healing again. In rapid succession He heals a leper, the centurion's servant, Peter's mother-in-law, then a group described only as "many that were possessed with devils." In short, it says, He "healed all that were sick" (Matt. 8:16).

Driven to cross the Sea of Galilee by the crowds that now

swarmed around Him, He cast devils out of two who were dwelling in the Gadarene tombs and then sailed back to "his own city" (Matt. 9:1), where He healed a man confined to bed with palsy, healed a woman with a twelve-year issue of blood (in what I think is one of the sweetest and most remarkable moments in all of the New Testament), and then raised the ruler's daughter from the dead—only, by the way, after dismissing the sideshow-seeking audience from the room.

Then He restored the sight of two blind men, followed by the casting out of a devil which had robbed a man of the ability to speak. That is a quick summary of the first five chapters in the New Testament devoted to Christ's ministry. Then this verse. See if it has an echo for you:

"And Jesus went about all the cities and villages, *teaching* in their synagogues, and *preaching* the gospel of the kingdom, and *healing* every sickness and every disease among the people" (Matt. 9:35; emphasis added).

That is, of course, except for a few words, exactly the verse we read five chapters earlier. And He needs help.

"But when he saw the multitudes, he was moved with compassion on them, because they fainted, and were scattered abroad, as sheep having no shepherd.

"Then saith he unto his disciples, The harvest truly is plenteous, but the labourers are few;

"Pray ye therefore the Lord of the harvest, that he will send forth labourers into his harvest" (Matt. 9:36–38).

With that He calls the Twelve and charges them with this directive: "Go," He says, "to the lost sheep of the house of Israel.

"And as ye go, preach, saying, The kingdom of heaven is at hand.

"Heal the sick, cleanse the lepers, raise the dead, cast out devils: freely ye have received, freely give" (Matt. 10:6–8; emphasis added).

Now, after taking too much time to make this point, let me make it. We know the Savior to be the Master Teacher. He is that and more. And when He says the bulk of the harvest yet lies before us and that there are far too few laborers, we immediately think of missionaries and others, like you, who need to teach. But the call is for a certain kind of teacher, a teacher who in the process heals.

Let me make myself absolutely clear. By "healing," as I have been speaking of it, I am *not* talking about formal use of the priesthood, or administration of the sick, or any such thing as that. That is not the role of those called as teachers in our Church organizations.

But I do believe Christ wants our teaching to lead to healing of the spiritual kind. I cannot believe that the ten chapters we have just referenced, of only twenty-eight that Matthew wrote, could be focused so much on the context of the Savior's ministry to distressed people, troubled people, distraught people if it were for no purpose. As with the Master, wouldn't it be wonderful to measure the success of your teaching by the healing that takes place in the lives of your students?

Let me be a little more specific. Rather than just giving a lesson, please try a little harder to help that blind basketball star really see, or the deaf homecoming queen really hear, or the privately lame student body president really walk. Try a little harder to fortify someone so powerfully that whatever temptations the devils of hell throw at her or him, these students will be able to withstand and thus truly in that moment be free from evil. Can you try a little harder to teach so powerfully and so

31

spiritually that you can take that student—that boy or girl who walks alone to school and from school, who sits alone in the lunchroom, who has never had a date, who is the brunt of every joke, who weeps in the dark of the night—can you unleash the power in the scriptures and the power in the gospel and "cleanse" that leper, a leper not of his or her making, a leper made by those on our right and on our left and sometimes by us?

Perhaps a lesson from contemporary life in the Quorum of the Twelve will help me say what I want to say on this point. I have suggested reading for a broad view, a "big picture," to see teachings in context. I have just used one example, not the best example, just an example. Now I want to turn that into an outcome, a teacher's assessment.

President Boyd K. Packer, himself a master teacher and long-time administrator in the Church Educational System, has a question he often asks when we have made a presentation or given some sort of exhortation to one another in the Twelve. He looks up as if to say, "Are you through?" And then says to the speaker (and, by implication, to the rest of the group), "Therefore, what?"

"Therefore, what?" I think that is what the Savior answered day in and day out as an inseparable element of His teaching and preaching. I've tried to suggest that. These sermons and exhortations were to no avail if the actual lives of His disciples did not change.

"Therefore, what?" You and I know that we still have young people, and too many older ones as well, who have not made the connection between what they say they believe and how they actually live their lives. Some, certainly not all and certainly not most, but some seem to be able to come from good homes, with the boys being graded up in the priesthood, and both the girls and boys advancing through the various Church programs, sometimes getting (and here I wish to be very care-ful) even to the temple for missions and marriage and those sacred covenants, only to discover that almost none of what they had been taught earlier—or at least not enough of it—had been translated into true repentance and gospel living.

Again I stress that I am speaking of exceptions. But some days it seems that there are more exceptions than either you or I or our Father in Heaven would like. So I reissue the call of the Master to have more laborers in the vineyard, not only declar-ing the gospel of the kingdom, but teaching in such a way that heals all manner of sickness among the people.

Pray that your teaching will bring change. Pray that, like the lyrics of a now-forgotten song, your lessons will literally cause a student to "straighten up and fly right."[2] We want them straight, and we want them right. We want them happy, happy in this life and saved in the world to come.

May I refer in quick succession to a few other "big picture" ideas, shifting significantly?

The book of Acts, which introduces the post-resurrection portion of the New Testament, is technically called "The Acts of the Apostles." That is an important ecclesiastical idea in the book, namely that the Apostles were ordained representatives of the Lord Jesus Christ and were thus authorized to lead the Church.

But consider what they faced. Consider the plight, the fear, the absolute confusion, the devastation of the members of the new little Christian Church after Christ was crucified. They may have understood something of what was happening, but they couldn't have understood it all. The people must have been very fearful and very confused, and the Brethren had their hands full trying to provide leadership.

The only contemporary example I can think of—and *please* do not misunderstand the comparison—might be the confusion and fear that reigned in our day after the martyrdom of the Prophet Joseph Smith. No one had had to face such a thought before. No one had even considered the Church without Joseph as its prophet. And now this. It was a moment of almost spiritual bedlam in Nauvoo.

But God did something that taught a great lesson to the people. To counter Sidney Rigdon and a few others vying for the prophetic office, the Lord made His will and power manifest in the matter as Brigham Young was transformed in visage and countenance before the people. You know the story very well. By momentarily giving Brigham Young Joseph's appearance and very manner of speech—quite literally his mantle— God said to the people, "The keys of the kingdom are with the Twelve. Brigham is Joseph's rightful successor in leading the Church."

That is the obvious and very important declaration about Church governance that the Lord was making. But an even more important declaration was the manifestation of heavenly power itself. God's might and direct involvement in this issue was the truly important thing that was conveyed here—not that Brigham Young was to be in charge or even that Joseph Smith had been in charge. The message was: *God is in charge*.

That is exactly the point being made in the book of Acts. Your students will not find that if you do not help them look for it. It is called "The Acts of the Apostles," and understandably so. It leads us to great respect for Peter, Paul, John, and the others. But not surprisingly, from the outset, from the first verse, the declaration is that the Church will continue to be *divinely* led, not mortally led. And that was important for them to hear in that hour of terrible confusion and fear. Indeed, a more complete title for the book of Acts could appropriately be something like "The Acts of the Resurrected Christ Working through the Holy Spirit in the Lives and Ministries of His Ordained Apostles." Now, having said that, you can see why someone voted for the shorter title—but my suggested title is more accurate! Listen to Luke's opening lines. That is exactly what he said. These are lines you all know:

"The former treatise have I made, O Theophilus, of all that Jesus began both to do and teach,

"Until the day in which he was taken up, *after that he through the Holy Ghost had given commandments unto the apostles whom he had chosen*" (Acts 1:1–2; emphasis added).

The direction of the Church is the same. The location of the Savior has been altered, but the direction and leadership of the Church is exactly the same. Then, having made that point, as if to prove in this most remarkable string of spiritual experiences all the way through the book, we get manifestations of the Lord's power through the Holy Ghost at every turn. It is, so to speak, the transformation of Brigham Young again and again. The first teaching in the book of Acts from the resurrected Christ to the Twelve is that they "shall be baptized with the Holy Ghost not many days hence" (Acts 1:5), and that "ye shall receive power, *after that the Holy Ghost is come upon you*" (v. 8; emphasis added).

After He ascended to heaven before their very eyes, Peter brought the Church together—all one hundred and twenty of them. Can you see what an impact the troubles and the Crucifixion and the opposition had had on them? One hundred and twenty people gathered, and Peter said, "Men and brethren, this scripture must needs have been fulfilled, which the *Holy Ghost* by the mouth of David spake before concerning Judas" (Acts 1:16; emphasis added). In filling Judas's vacancy in the Twelve, they prayed exactly the way the Quorum of the Twelve and First Presidency pray today: "*Thou, Lord,* which knowest the hearts of all men, shew whether of these . . . thou hast chosen" (v. 24; emphasis added). "Shew whether of these . . . *thou hast chosen.*" And Matthias was called.

But that first chapter of turning heavenward, so clearly marking the divine guidance that would continue to direct the Church, is only a warm-up to chapter 2. In those passages, the very name *Pentecost* comes into the Christian vocabulary as synonymous with breathtaking spiritual manifestations and a divine outpouring of the Holy Ghost upon all the people. Revelation came from heaven with the sound "as of a rushing mighty wind, and it filled all the house" (Acts 2:2), and it filled the Brethren. "There appeared unto them cloven tongues like as of fire. . . . *And they were all filled with the Holy Ghost, and began to speak . . . as the Spirit gave them utterance*" (vv. 3–4; emphasis added).

Peter, as chief Apostle and President of the Church, stood and acknowledged this outpouring. He quoted Joel, whom Moroni would also quote later, saying that God would in the last days "*pour out of my Spirit upon all flesh:* and your sons and your daughters shall prophesy, and your young men shall see visions, and your old men shall dream dreams:

"And on my servants and on my handmaidens *I will pour out in those days of my Spirit;* and they shall prophesy" (Acts 2:17–18; emphasis added).

Peter continued: "Ye men of Israel [he's speaking to the

larger congregation], hear these words; Jesus of Nazareth, a man approved of God among you. . . .

"This Jesus hath God raised up, . . . by the right hand of God exalted, and *having received of the Father the promise of the Holy Ghost,* he hath shed forth this, which ye now see and hear" (Acts 2:22, 32–33; emphasis added).

It is a magnificent passage. Those not yet baptized that day, moved by this Spirit, asked what they should do. Peter told them to be baptized for the remission of sins and to *"receive the gift of the Holy Ghost"* (Acts 2:38; emphasis added), and three thousand of them did so. Later when the lame man was raised to health on the steps of the temple and the crowd thought Peter and John had done something wonderful, Peter chided them, chastised them, said it was not their mortal power or any holiness from them that made the man to walk, but rather that of Jesus, whom they had "delivered up" and "killed" (Acts 3:13, 15)—that's his phrase. He said this same Jesus was still leading the Church through the instrumentality of the Holy Spirit and would continue to do so until He came again in "the times of restitution of all things" (v. 21).

When this time five thousand people joined the Church, the local Pharisees and Sadducees were stunned. These Jewish leaders demanded to know how all of this was being done. Peter gave the classic answer you must always give your students. *"Filled with the Holy Ghost,"* the scripture says, he declared that it was done in and "by the name of Jesus Christ of Nazareth" (Acts 4:8, 10). Christ directing His apostles through the Holy Spirit—a near perfect vignette, repeated again and again, of that eternal principle. Your students will not see these things if you do not point them out to them. They will not read with that imagination and insight without a teacher's help. It is a great lesson about the modern governance of The Church of Jesus Christ of Latter-day Saints.

As we leave this point, let these phrases run through your mind and see if you get the picture:

"They were all filled with the Holy Ghost, and they spake the word of God with boldness" (Acts 4:31).

"Ananias, why hath Satan filled thine heart to lie to the Holy Ghost?" (Acts 5:3).

"We are his witnesses of these things; and so is also the Holy Ghost" (Acts 5:32).

"They chose Stephen, a man full of faith and of the Holy Ghost" (Acts 6:5).

"He, being full of the Holy Ghost, looked up stedfastly into heaven" (Acts 7:55).

"Peter and John . . . prayed for them, that they might receive the Holy Ghost. . . . Then laid they their hands on them, and they received the Holy Ghost" (Acts 8:14–15, 17).

"Then the Spirit said unto Philip, Go near. . . . And when they were come up out of the water, the Spirit of the Lord caught away Philip" (Acts 8:29, 39).

Well, we could go on into exhaustion or your boredom or both. In any case we have scarcely made it to Acts 8, with all the revelation and spiritual manifestation of Paul's conversion and ministry, the larger part of the story, yet to come. As you read this account, note that everything makes this affirmation— that the Father and the Son direct this work still, largely having their impact upon individuals and Church leaders through the means of the Holy Ghost. And it is through that same instrumentality that we must have our impact in our service.

Please teach by the Holy Spirit. If we do not teach that way, then by scriptural definition we are teaching "some other way"

(D&C 50:17). And any other way "is not of God" (v. 20). Give your students a spiritual experience in every way that you can. That is what the New Testament is trying to do for you. That is the message of the Gospels. It is the message of the book of Acts. It is the message of all scripture. Those spiritual experiences from those sacred records will keep your students on track and in the Church in our day just as they did in the early days of those members in New Testament times, and just as they have done in every other dispensation of time.

"The Spirit shall be given unto you by the prayer of faith; and if ye receive not the Spirit ye shall not teach" (D&C 42:14). Not just that you won't teach or that you can't teach or that it will be pretty shoddy teaching. No, it is stronger than that. It is the imperative form of the verb: "Ye *shall not* teach." Put a *thou* in there for *ye* and you have Mt. Sinai language. This is a commandment. These are God's students, not yours, just like it is God's Church, not Peter or Paul or Joseph or Brigham's.

Facilitate that manifestation in the hearts of your young people, which lets them know where power, safety, and salvation really are, through the instrumentality of these our Church leaders and the blessings of Church life. Have them look to heaven for their guidance just as the eleven did that day Christ ascended from the Mount of Olives before their very eyes, just as Peter did that day when he led them in prayer to fill the vacancy in the Twelve, just as the early Saints did in seeing Brigham Young transformed before their eyes.

Let me close. I remember almost dreading (I think that's not too strong a word) the responsibility to teach the Crucifixion, Atonement, and Resurrection in my classes because I never felt I could rise to the level of worthiness that I knew the subject deserved. I wanted so much for it to matter in the hearts of the

39

students, and I knew if there was a weak link in the experience, it wouldn't be the student and it surely wouldn't be the Lord— it would be me.

Although I love the Savior even more now and have been called to be a witness of His name in all the world, still I feel overwhelmed and inadequate on this topic. I say that to encourage you. You as teachers will feel that some days, and often it will be the days when you want to be your best.

Take heart. Let the Spirit work in you in ways that you may not be privileged to see or even to recognize. More will go on than you think if you are honest in your heart and trying to live as purely as you can. When you get to those supreme and nearly impossible-to-teach moments of Gethsemane and Calvary and the Ascension, I would ask that you remember, among many things, two of the many applications that I would hope you would make with your students.

Remind the students, and there is so much else to say, but remind the students that in this unspeakably wrenching and nature-shattering pain, *Christ remained true*.

Matthew said He was "sorrowful and very heavy . . . exceeding sorrowful, even unto death" (Matt. 26:37–38). He went alone into the garden, intentionally left the Brethren outside to wait. He had to do this alone. He dropped to His knees and then, the Apostle says, He "fell on his face" (v. 39). Luke says He was "in an agony" and prayed so earnestly His sweat became "great drops of blood falling down to the ground" (Luke 22:44). Mark says He fell and cried, "Abba, Father" (Mark 14:36). *Papa*, we would say, or *Daddy*. This is not abstract theology now. This is a Boy pleading with His Dad. "Abba [Daddy, Papa] . . . all things are possible unto thee; take away this cup from me."

40

Who could resist that? God in His heavens—in His righteousness, for this, His only perfect child—who could resist? "You can do anything. I know you can do anything. Take this cup from me."

That whole prayer, Mark noted, had been that if it were possible, this hour would be stricken from the plan. He says, in effect, "If there is another path, I would rather walk it. If there is any other way—any other way—I will gladly embrace it." "Let this cup pass from me," Matthew says (Matt. 26:39). "Remove this cup from me," says Luke (Luke 22:42). But in the end, the cup does not pass.

Then He said and did that which most characterizes His life in time and in eternity, the words and the act that distinguish Jesus as the Son of God, according to the great Book of Mormon prophet Abinadi. He said and did what He had to do to fulfill His destiny as the Son (with a capital S). He yielded to the will of His Father and said, "Not my will, but thine, be done" (Luke 22:42). That is, for all intents and purposes, the last moment in the divine conversation between Father and Son in Jesus' mortal ministry. From there on the die has been cast. He will see it through no matter what.

And from that last declaration in the Old World, we get this first declaration in the New. To the Nephites gathered at the temple, He would say, "Behold, I am Jesus Christ, . . . the light and the life of the world; and I have drunk out of that bitter cup which the Father hath given me, and . . . I have suffered the will of the Father in all things from the beginning" (3 Nephi 11:10–11). That is His own introduction of Himself, the declaration He feels best tells us who He is.

If you can leave your students one element of commitment in response to the Savior's incomparable sacrifice for them, His payment for their transgressions, His sorrow for their sins, try to help them see the necessity to obey—in their own difficult domain and hours of decision, to yield, to suffer "the will of the Father" (3 Ne. 11:11), whatever the cost. They won't always do that, any better than you and I have been able to do it, but that ought to be their goal; that ought to be their aim. The thing Christ seems most anxious to stress about His mission—beyond the personal virtues and beyond the magnificent sermons and even beyond the healing—is that He submitted His will to the will of the Father.

We are all willful people, maybe too much of the time. Certainly your students can be willful as they test the water, test the limits, test their faith and the Church, and, often enough, your faith. But the message for every one of us and every one of them is that our offering, in similitude of His offering, is a broken heart and a contrite spirit. We must break out of our petty selves and weep for our sins and for the sins of the world. Plead with your students to yield to the Father, to yield to the Son, to yield to the Holy Spirit. There is no other way. Without likening ourselves to Him too much, because that would be sacrilegious to do, nevertheless that symbol of the cup that cannot pass is a cup that comes in our life as well as in His. It is in a much lesser way, to a much lesser degree, but it comes often enough to teach us that we have to obey.

The second lesson of the Atonement that I would ask you to remember for and with your students is related. If your students feel that they have somehow made too many mistakes already, if they feel they have turned their backs on the principle of obedience one too many times, if they feel that they work and live and labor lower than the light of Christ can shine, teach them, as the Prophet Joseph shared with the

Saints, that God has "a forgiving disposition," that Christ is "merciful and gracious, slow to anger, long-suffering and full of goodness."[3] Mercy, with its sister virtues of repentance and forgiveness, is at the very heart of the Atonement of Jesus Christ. Everything in the gospel teaches us that we can change if we really want to, that we can be helped if we truly ask for it, that we can be made whole, whatever the problems of the past.

In spite of life's tribulations and as fearful as some of their prospects are, there is help for your students on this journey. When Christ bids them to yield, to submit, to obey the Father, He knows how to help them do that. He has walked that way, asking them to do what He has done. He has made it safer. He has made it very much easier for their travel and ours. He knows where the sharp stones and the stumbling blocks lie and where the thorns and the thistles are the most severe. He knows where the path is perilous, and He knows which way to go when the road forks and nightfall comes. He knows this because He has suffered "pains and afflictions and temptations of every kind . . . that he may know . . . how to succor his people according to their infirmities" (Alma 7:11–12). To succor means "to run to." Testify to your students that Christ will run to them, and is running even now, if they will but receive the extended arms of His mercy.

To those who stagger or stumble, He is there to steady and strengthen us. In the end He is there to save us, and for all this He gave His life. However dim our days or your students' days may seem, they have been a lot darker for the Savior of the world. As a reminder of those days, Jesus has chosen, even in a resurrected, otherwise perfected body, to retain for the benefit of His disciples the wounds in His hands and in His feet and in His side—signs, if you will, that painful things happen even to the pure and the perfect; signs, if you will, that pain in this world is *not* evidence that God doesn't love you; signs, if you will, that problems pass and happiness can be ours. Remind your students that it is the wounded Christ who is the Captain of our souls, He who yet bears the scars of our forgiveness, the lesions of His love and humility, the torn flesh of obedience and sacrifice.

These wounds are the principal way we are to recognize Him when He comes. He may invite us forward, as He has invited others, to see and to feel those marks. If not before, then surely at that time, we will remember with Isaiah that it was for us that a God was "despised and rejected . . . ; a man of sorrows, and acquainted with grief," that "he was wounded for our trans-gressions, he was bruised for our iniquities: the chastisement of our peace was upon him; and with his stripes we are healed" (Isa. 53:3, 5).

I testify that Jesus Christ is the Son of God. I testify that He is perfect, one with His Father in every thought, every virtue, every deed, every desire. I testify that His is the greatest life ever lived and that in His name only is salvation.

Notes

From an address given at the Twenty-fourth Annual Church Educational System religious educators conference held at Brigham Young University, 8 August 2000.

1. Charles Dickens, A Tale of Two Cities (New York: Oxford University Press, 1988), 1.
2. Nat King Cole, "Straighten Up and Fly Right" (1943).
3. Joseph Smith, Lectures on Faith (Salt Lake City: Deseret Book, 1985), 42.

5

MISSIONARY WORK
AND THE ATONEMENT

The Prophet Joseph Smith once declared that all things "which pertain to our religion are only appendages" to the Atonement of Jesus Christ.[1] In like manner and for the same reasons, every truth that a missionary or member teaches is only an appendage to the central message of all time—that Jesus is the Christ, the Only Begotten Son of God, the Holy Messiah, the Promised One, the Savior and Redeemer of the world; that He alone burst the bands of death and triumphed over the captivity of hell; that no one of us could ever have those same blessings without His intervention in our behalf; and that there never shall be any "other name given nor any other way nor means whereby salvation can come unto the children of men, [except] in and through the name of Christ, the Lord Omnipotent" (Mosiah 3:17; see Acts 4:12).

Our basic message is that with a complete offering of His body, His blood, and the anguish of His spirit, Christ atoned for the initial transgression of Adam and Eve in the Garden of Eden, and also for the personal sins of everyone else who would ever live in this world from Adam to the end of time.

Some of those blessings are unconditional, such as the gift of the Resurrection. Other blessings, at least the full realization of them, are very conditional, requiring the keeping of commandments, the performance of ordinances, and living the life of a disciple of Christ.

Either way, the essential message of the gospel, the starting point for all other truths, is this from the Master's own lips: "I am the way, the truth, and the life: no man cometh unto the Father, but by me" (John 14:6). Thus the Atonement of Christ, which makes that return to the Father possible, is rightfully seen as the central fact, the crucial foundation, and the chief doctrine of the great and eternal plan of salvation—"our Heavenly Father's plan," which we are called to teach.

Little wonder, then, that the Apostle Paul, the greatest missionary the world has ever known (or at least one of them), said: "The preaching of the cross is to them that perish foolishness; but unto us which are saved it is the power of God. . . . For the Jews require a sign, and the Greeks seek after wisdom: *But we preach Christ crucified*" (1 Cor. 1:18, 22–23; emphasis added).

Inherent in all of this is a rather simple definition of the gospel, at least when considered in its essence. The word *gospel* as we use it in English comes down to us through early scriptural language which meant literally "good news" or, sometimes, "glad tidings." The "good news" was that death and hell could be escaped, that mistakes and sins could be overcome, that there was hope, that there was help, that the insoluble was solved, that the enemy had been conquered. The "good news" was that *everyone's* tomb could one day be empty, that *everyone's* soul could again be pure, that *every* child of God could again return to the Father who gave them life.

This is the essence of the message delivered by every prophet who has ever lived and every Apostle ever called to the work. It is the message we are called to declare. It is the message of the angel who came to those unsuspecting Judean shepherds:

"And, lo, the angel of the Lord came upon them, and the glory of the Lord shone round about them: and they were sore afraid.

"And the angel said unto them, Fear not: for, behold, *I bring you good tidings of great joy* [or, in other words, I bring you the *gospel* personified], which shall be to all people.

"For unto you is born this day in the city of David a Saviour, which is Christ the Lord" (Luke 2:9–11; emphasis added).

Probably there are very few missionaries, if any, who do not know the centrality of this doctrine. But I have been surprised to regularly be with the missionaries and discover that this is not something that readily comes forward in a discussion of missionary work.

For example, in zone conferences, which are some of the greatest teaching moments we as General Authorities have with these young elders and sisters, I have asked missionaries what it is they want investigators to do as a result of their discussions with them.

"Be baptized!" is shouted forward in an absolute chorus.

"Yes," I say, "we do want them to be baptized, but what has to precede that?"

Now they are a little leery. *Aha*, they think. *This is a test. It is a test on the first discussion.* "Read the Book of Mormon!" someone shouts. "Pray!" an elder roars from the back of the room.

"Attend church!" one of the sisters on the front row declares. "Receive all of the discussions!" someone else offers.

"Well, you have pretty much covered the commitments in the first discussion," I say, "but what else do you want your investigators to do?"

"Be baptized!" The chorus comes a second time.

"Elders," I plead, "you have already told me about baptism, and I am still asking!"

Well, now they *are* stumped. *It must be commitments from the other discussions,* they think. "Live the Word of Wisdom!" someone says. "Pay tithing!" another shouts. And so it goes.

I don't always run through this little exercise in a zone conference, but sometimes I do. And I have to say that almost never do the missionaries get around to identifying the two most fundamental things we want investigators to do prior to baptism: have faith in the Lord Jesus Christ and repent of their sins. Yet "we believe that the first principles and ordinances of the Gospel are: first, Faith in the Lord Jesus Christ; second, Repentance; [*then*] third, Baptism by immersion *for the remission of sins*; fourth, Laying on of hands for the gift of the Holy Ghost" (A of F 1:4; emphasis added).

A convert's new life is to be built upon faith in the Lord Jesus Christ and His redeeming sacrifice—a conviction that He really is the Son of God, that He lives this very moment, that He really is the door of the sheepfold, that He alone holds the key to our salvation and exaltation. That belief is to be followed by true repentance, repentance which shows our desire to be clean and renewed and whole, repentance that allows us to lay claim to the full blessings of the Atonement.

Then comes baptism for the remission of sins. Yes, baptism is also for membership in the Church, but that isn't what the

Prophet Joseph Smith chose to stress in that article of faith. He stressed that it was baptism for the remission of sins—focusing you and me, the missionary and the investigator, again on the Atonement, on salvation, on the gift Christ gives us. This points that new convert toward the blessings of the "good news."

In an effort to keep our work closely linked to the Savior's ministry, let me suggest some things all of us might do to keep Christ and His Atonement in the forefront of members' and investigators' consciousness.

Encourage in every way possible more spiritual Church meetings, especially sacrament meetings. One of the great fears missionaries have, at least in some locations, is taking their investigators to church. And indeed the investigators deserve to feel essentially the same spirit in sacrament meeting that they feel when being taught by the missionaries.

It will also help orient investigators if missionaries will take some time to explain the ordinance of the sacrament that investigators will be witnessing, what it means for the renewing of baptismal covenants, that the emblems represent the Savior's body and blood, and so forth. Missionaries could read to these investigators the sacramental prayers as found in the scriptures, they could share some of the words of favorite sacrament hymns, or they could do any number of other things that would help these new visitors and prospective members have a powerful learning experience when they visit a sacrament meeting.

In like manner, do all that you can to make your baptismal services a spiritual, Christ-centered experience. A new convert deserves to have this be a sacred, carefully planned, and spiritually uplifting moment. The prayers, the hymns, surely the talks that are given—all ought to be focused on the significance of

49

this ordinance and the Atonement of Christ, which makes it efficacious.

Probably no other meeting we hold in the Church has the high referral and future baptismal harvest that a baptismal service does. Many of the investigators who attend a baptismal service (that is, the service of someone else being baptized) will go on to their own baptisms. That is more likely to occur if this service is a spiritual, strong teaching moment in which it is clear to participants and visitors alike that this is a sacred act of faith centered on the Lord Jesus Christ, that it is an act of repentance claiming the cleansing power of Christ, that through His majesty and Atonement it brings a remission of sins as well as, with confirmation, membership in His Church. Missionaries, don't get so consumed with the desire to record a baptism that you yourselves forget what this baptism represents and what it must mean in the life of this new member.

Throughout the teaching experience, missionaries must bear testimony of the Savior and His gift of salvation to us. Obviously you should bear testimony regularly of all the principles you are teaching, but it is especially important that you bear testimony of this central doctrine in the plan of our Heavenly Father.

There are several reasons for bearing testimony. One is that when you declare the truth, it will bring an echo, a memory, even if it is an unconscious memory, to the investigator, that they have heard this truth before—and of course they have. A missionary's testimony invokes a great legacy of testimony dating back to the councils in heaven before this world was. There, in an earlier place, these same people heard this same plan outlined and heard there the role that Jesus Christ would play in their salvation.

"And I heard a loud voice saying in heaven, Now is come salvation, and strength, and the kingdom of our God, and *the power of his Christ:* for the accuser of our brethren is cast down, which accused them before our God day and night.

"*And they overcame him by the blood of the Lamb, and by the word of their testimony;* and they loved not their lives unto the death" (Rev. 12:10–11; emphasis added).

So the fact of the matter is investigators are not only hearing our testimony of Christ, but they are hearing echoes of other, earlier testimonies, including their own testimony of Him, for they were on the side of the faithful who kept their first estate and earned the privilege of a second estate. We must always remember that these investigators—every man, woman, and child—were among the valiant who once overcame Satan by the power of their testimony of Christ! So when they hear others bear that witness of Christ's saving mission, it has a familiar feeling; it brings an echo of truth they themselves already know.

Furthermore, when you bear witness of "Jesus Christ, and him crucified," to use Paul's phrase (1 Cor. 2:2), you invoke the power of God the Father and the Holy Ghost. The Savior Himself taught about bearing witness before any other doctrine when He visited the Nephites:

"After this manner shall ye baptize in my name; for behold, verily I say unto you, that the Father, and the Son, and the Holy Ghost are one. . . .

"And this is my doctrine, and it is the doctrine which the Father hath given unto me. . . .

" . . . Whoso believeth in me believeth in the Father also; and *unto him* [the investigator] *will the Father bear record of me, for he will visit him* [the investigator] *with fire and with the Holy Ghost.*

"And thus will the Father bear record of me, and the Holy Ghost will bear record unto him [the investigator] of the Father and me; for the Father, and I, and the Holy Ghost are one.

" . . . This is my doctrine, and whoso buildeth upon this buildeth upon my rock, and the gates of hell shall not prevail against them" (3 Ne. 11:27, 32, 35–36, 39; emphasis added).

So why should we bear frequent and powerful testimony of Christ as Savior, as Redeemer, as atoning Lamb of God? Because doing so invites and becomes part of the divine power of testimony borne by God the Father and by the Holy Ghost, a testimony borne on wings of fire to the very hearts of investigators. Such a divine testimony of Christ is the rock upon which every new convert must build. Only this testimony of the atoning Anointed, Victorious One will prevail against the gates of hell. So saith the Son of God Himself.

Study the scriptures conscientiously and become familiar with those passages that teach and testify of Christ's redeeming mission. Nothing will so touch your heart and stir your soul like the truths of which I have been speaking.

I would particularly ask full-time and member missionaries to study from and teach the Atonement of Christ out of the Book of Mormon. I say that in a very biased way, because it was on my own mission that I came to love the Book of Mormon and the majesty of the Son of God which is revealed there. In its unparalleled focus on the messianic message of the Savior of the world, the Book of Mormon is literally a new testament or (to avoid confusion) "another testament" of Jesus Christ. As such the book centers upon that which scriptural testaments have always centered upon since the days of Adam and Eve: the declaration to all that through the Atonement of the Son of God, "as thou hast fallen thou mayest be redeemed, and all mankind, even as many as will" (Moses 5:9).

There is not enough space here to convey the wonder and breadth of these Book of Mormon sermons, but consider this from Nephi early in his ministry:

"And the world, because of their iniquity, shall judge him to be a thing of naught; wherefore they scourge him, and he suffereth it; and they smite him, and he suffereth it. Yea, they spit upon him, and he suffereth it, because of his loving kindness and his long-suffering towards the children of men.

"And the God of our fathers, . . . yea, the God of Abraham, and of Isaac, and the God of Jacob, yieldeth himself . . . as a man, into the hands of wicked men, to be lifted up, according to the words of Zenock, and to be crucified, according to the words of Neum, and to be buried in a sepulchre, according to the words of Zenos. . . .

"And all these things must surely come, saith the prophet Zenos. And the rocks of the earth must rend; and because of the groanings of the earth, many of the kings of the isles of the sea shall be wrought upon by the Spirit of God, to exclaim: The God of nature suffers" (1 Ne. 19:9–10, 12).

Or this from Nephi at the end of his life:

"And now, my beloved brethren, after ye have gotten into this strait and narrow path, I would ask if all is done? Behold, I say unto you, Nay; for ye have not come thus far save it were by the word of Christ with unshaken faith in him, relying wholly upon the merits of him who is mighty to save.

"Wherefore, ye must press forward with a steadfastness in Christ, having a perfect brightness of hope, and a love of God and of all men. Wherefore, if ye shall press forward, feasting upon the word of Christ, and endure to the end, behold, thus saith the Father: Ye shall have eternal life.

"And now, behold, my beloved brethren, this is the way; . . . this is the doctrine of Christ, and the only and true doctrine of the Father, and of the Son, and of the Holy Ghost" (2 Ne. 31:19–21).

Or this from Nephi's remarkable brother Jacob, who gave a *two-day* sermon on the Fall and the Atonement!

"I know . . . that in the body he shall show himself unto those at Jerusalem . . . ; for it behooveth the great Creator that he suffereth himself to become subject unto man in the flesh, and die for all men, that all men might become subject unto him.

"For as death hath passed upon all men, to fulfil the merciful plan of the great Creator, there must needs be a power of resurrection, and the resurrection must needs come unto man by reason of the fall; and the fall came by reason of transgression; and because man became fallen they were cut off from the presence of the Lord.

"Wherefore, it must needs be an infinite atonement. . . .

"O how great the goodness of our God, who prepareth a way for our escape from the grasp of this awful monster; yea, that monster, death and hell, which I call the death of the body, and also the death of the spirit. . . .

"And he cometh into the world that he may save all men if they will hearken unto his voice; for behold, he suffereth the pains of all men, yea, the pains of every living creature, both men, women, and children, who belong to the family of Adam.

"And he suffereth this that the resurrection might pass upon all men. . . .

"And he commandeth all men that they must repent, and

be baptized in his name, having perfect faith in the Holy One of Israel, or they cannot be saved in the kingdom of God" (2 Ne. 9:5–7, 10, 21–23).

Consider this from King Benjamin:

"For behold, the time cometh, and is not far distant, that with power, the Lord Omnipotent . . . shall come down from heaven among the children of men, and shall dwell in a tabernacle of clay, and shall go forth amongst men, working mighty miracles, such as healing the sick, raising the dead, causing the lame to walk, the blind to receive their sight, and the deaf to hear, and curing all manner of diseases.

"And he shall cast out devils, or the evil spirits which dwell in the hearts of the children of men.

"And lo, he shall suffer temptations, and pain of body, hunger, thirst, and fatigue, even more than man can suffer, except it be unto death; for behold, blood cometh from every pore, so great shall be his anguish for the wickedness and the abominations of his people.

" . . . And even after all this they shall consider him a man, and say that he hath a devil, and shall scourge him, and shall crucify him.

"And he shall rise the third day from the dead. . . .

" . . . His blood atoneth for the sins of those who have fallen by the transgression of Adam, who have died not knowing the will of God concerning them, or who have ignorantly sinned" (Mosiah 3:5–7, 9–11).

Or, as a last example, this from the great patriarch Lehi:

"Wherefore, redemption cometh in and through the Holy Messiah. . . .

"Behold, he offereth himself a sacrifice for sin, to answer the ends of the law, unto all those who have a broken heart and a contrite spirit; and unto none else can the ends of the law be answered.

"Wherefore, *how great the importance to make these things known unto the inhabitants of the earth,* that they may know that there is no flesh that can dwell in the presence of God, save it be through the merits, and mercy, and grace of the Holy Messiah, who layeth down his life according to the flesh, and taketh it again by the power of the Spirit, that he may bring to pass the resurrection of the dead, being the first that should rise.

"Wherefore, he is the firstfruits unto God, inasmuch as he shall make intercession for all the children of men; and they that believe in him shall be saved" (2 Ne. 2:6–9; emphasis added).

Obviously you recognize that these samples are testimonies from just the first pages of the Book of Mormon. Perhaps this is enough to give you a feel for the urgent, impressive theme that runs all through that sacred record. With its declared title-page purpose of testifying that Jesus is the Christ, little wonder that the Book of Mormon was the first—and is still the greatest—missionary tract of this dispensation. As Lehi says to me and to you, "How great the importance to make these things [of the Atonement] known unto the inhabitants of the earth."

I testify to you that we will change lives, including our own, if we will teach the Atonement from the Book of Mormon, as well as, of course, from all of the other scriptures.

Almost everything I have said here has been an aid directed toward the missionary process, ultimately toward the investigator. May I close with an extended testimony about how focusing on the Atonement helps full-time and member missionaries and mission leaders.

Anyone who does any kind of missionary work will have

occasion to ask, Why is this so hard? Why doesn't it go better? Why can't our success be more rapid? Why aren't there more people joining the Church? It is the truth. We believe in angels. We trust in miracles. Why don't people just flock to the font? Why isn't the only risk in missionary work that of pneumonia from being soaking wet all day and all night in the baptismal font?

You will have occasion to ask those questions. I have thought about this a great deal. I offer this as my personal feeling. I am convinced that missionary work is not easy because *salvation is not a cheap experience.* Salvation *never* was easy. We are The Church of Jesus Christ, this is the truth, and He is our Great Eternal Head. How could we believe it would be easy for us when it was never, ever easy for Him? It seems to me that missionaries and mission leaders have to spend at least a few moments in Gethsemane. Missionaries and mission leaders have to take at least a step or two toward the summit of Calvary.

Now, please don't misunderstand. I'm not talking about anything anywhere near what Christ experienced. That would be presumptuous and sacrilegious. But I believe that missionaries *and* investigators, to come to the truth, to come to salvation, to know something of this price that has been paid, will have to pay a token of that same price.

For that reason I don't believe missionary work has ever been easy, nor that conversion is, nor that retention is, nor that continued faithfulness is. I believe it is supposed to require some effort, something from the depths of our souls.

If He could come forward in the night, kneel down, fall on His face, bleed from every pore, and cry, "Abba, Father (Papa), if this cup can pass, let it pass" (see Mark 14:36), then little wonder that salvation is not a whimsical or easy thing for us.

If you wonder if there isn't an easier way, you should remember you are not the first one to ask that. Someone a lot greater and a lot grander asked a long time ago if there wasn't an easier way.

The Atonement will carry the missionaries perhaps even more importantly than it will carry the investigators. When you struggle, when you are rejected, when you are spit upon and cast out and made a hiss and a byword, you are standing with the best life this world has ever known, the only pure and perfect life ever lived. You have reason to stand tall and be grateful that the Living Son of the Living God knows all about your sorrows and afflictions. The only way to salvation is through Gethsemane and on to Calvary. The only way to eternity is through Him—the Way, the Truth, and the Life.

I testify that the living God is our Eternal Father and that Jesus Christ is His living and Only Begotten Son in the flesh. I testify that this Jesus, who was slain and hanged on a tree (see Acts 5:30), was the chief Apostle then and is the chief Apostle now, the Great High Priest, the chief cornerstone of His Church in this last and greatest of all dispensations. I testify that He lives, that the whole triumph of the gospel is that He lives, and because He does, so will we.

On that first Resurrection Sunday, Mary Magdalene first thought she saw a gardener. Well, she did—the Gardener who cultivated Eden and who endured Gethsemane. The Gardener who gave us the rose of Sharon, the lily of the valley, the cedars of Lebanon, the tree of life.

I declare Him to be the Savior of the world, the Bishop and Shepherd of our souls, the Bright and Morning Star. I know that our garments can be washed white only in the blood of that Lamb, slain from the foundation of the world. I know that we are lifted up unto life because He was lifted up unto death, that He bore our griefs and carried our sorrows, and with His stripes we are healed. I bear witness that He was wounded for our transgressions and bruised for our iniquities, that He was a man of sorrows acquainted with grief because upon Him were laid the transgressions of us all (see Isa. 53:3–6; Mosiah 14:3–6).

I bear witness that He came from God as a God to bind up the brokenhearted, to dry the tears from every eye, to proclaim liberty to the captives and open the prison doors to them that are bound (see Isa. 61:1). I promise that because of your faithful response to the call to spread the gospel, He will bind up *your* broken hearts, dry *your* tears, and set *you* and your families free. That is my missionary promise to you and your missionary message to the world.

Notes

From a talk given at the Provo (Utah) Missionary Training Center, 20 June 2000.

1.   Joseph Smith, *Teachings of the Prophet Joseph Smith*, sel. Joseph Fielding Smith (Salt Lake City: Deseret Book, 1976), 121.

CONFIDENT IN HIS CARE

6

"COME UNTO ME"

In the 11th chapter of Matthew, verses 28–30, the Savior says: "Come unto me, all ye that labour and are heavy laden, and I will give you rest. Take my yoke upon you, and learn of me; for I am meek and lowly in heart: and ye shall find rest unto your souls. For my yoke is easy, and my burden is light."

This is my basic message to each of you, wherever you live, whatever your joys or sorrows, however young or old you may be, at whatever point you may find yourself in this mortal journey of ours. Some of you are where you want to be, or you know where you want to go with your lives, and some of you don't. Some of you seem to have so many blessings and so many wonderful choices ahead of you. Others of you feel, for a time and for whatever reason, less fortunate and with fewer attractive paths lying immediately ahead.

But whoever you are and wherever you find yourself as you seek your way in life, I offer you "the way . . . and the life" (John

14:6). Wherever else you think you may be going, I ask you to "come unto Him" as the imperative first step in getting there, in finding your individual happiness and strength and success.

Beloved friends, I know of no other way for you to succeed or to be happy or to be safe. I know of no other way for you to be able to carry your burdens or find what Jacob called "that happiness which is prepared for the saints" (2 Ne. 9:43). That is why we make solemn covenants based on Christ's atoning sacrifice, and that is why we take upon us His name. In as many ways as possible, both figuratively and literally, we try to take upon us His identity. We seek out His teachings and retell His miracles. We send latter-day witnesses, including prophets, Apostles, and missionaries, around the world to declare His message. We call ourselves His children, and we testify that He is the only source of eternal life. We plead for Him to swing open the gates of heaven in our behalf, and we trust everlastingly that He will, based upon our faithfulness.

My desire for you is to have more straightforward experiences with the Savior's life and teachings. Perhaps sometimes we come to Christ too obliquely, focusing on structure or methods or elements of Church administration. Those are important and, like the tithes of mint and anise and cummin Christ spoke of (see Matt. 23:23), should be observed—but not without attention to the weightier matters of the kingdom, first and foremost of which is a personal spiritual relationship with Deity, including the Savior, whose kingdom this is.

The Prophet Joseph Smith taught in the *Lectures on Faith* that it is necessary to have "an acquaintance" (that's his phrase) with the divine attributes of the Father and the Son in order to have faith in them. Specifically, he said that unless we believe Christ to be "merciful and gracious, slow to anger, long-suffering and full of goodness"—unless we can rely on these unchanging attributes—we will never have the faith necessary to claim the blessings of heaven. If we cannot count on "the excellency of . . . character" (that is also his phrase) maintained by the Savior and His willingness and ability to "forgive iniquity, transgression, and sin," we will be, he said, "in constant doubt of salvation." But because the Father and the Son are unchangeably "full of goodness," then, in the words of the Prophet, such knowledge "does away [with] doubt, and makes faith exceedingly strong."[1]

I don't know what things may be troubling you personally, but, even knowing how terrific you are and how faithfully you are living, I would be surprised if someone somewhere weren't troubled by a transgression or the temptation of transgression. To you, wherever you may be, I say, Come unto Him and lay down your burden. Let Him lift the load. Let Him give peace to your soul. Nothing in this world is more burdensome than sin— it is the heaviest cross men and women ever bear.

The world around us is an increasingly hostile and sinful place. Occasionally that splashes onto us, and perhaps, in the case of a few of you, it may be nearly drowning you. To anyone struggling under the burden of sin, I say again with the Prophet Joseph that God has "a forgiving disposition."[2] You can change. You can be helped. You can be made whole—whatever the problem. All He asks is that you walk away from the darkness and come into the light, His light, with meekness and lowliness of heart. That is at the heart of the gospel. That is the very center of our message. That is the beauty of redemption. Christ has "borne our griefs, and carried our sorrows," Isaiah declared, "and with his stripes we are healed"—if we want to be (Isa. 53:4–5; Mosiah 14:4–5).

For anyone seeking the courage to repent and change, I remind you that the Church is not a monastery for the isolation of perfect people. It is more like a hospital provided for those who wish to get well. Do whatever you have to do to come into the fold and be blessed. For some of you that is simply to live with greater faith, to believe more. For some of you it does mean to repent—right here. Today. For some of you it means to be baptized and come into the body and fellowship of Christ. For virtually all of us it means to live more by the promptings and promises of the Holy Ghost and to "press forward with a steadfastness in Christ, having a perfect brightness of hope, and a love of God and of all men."

"This is the way," Nephi said—there is that word again—"and there is none other way . . . whereby man [or woman] can be saved in the kingdom of God" (2 Ne. 31:20–21).

This reliance upon the forgiving, long-suffering, merciful nature of God was taught from before the very foundation of the world. It was always to give us hope and help, a reason to progress and improve, an incentive to lay down our burdens and take up our salvation. May I be bold enough to suggest that it is impossible for anyone who really knows God to doubt His willingness to receive us with open arms in a divine embrace if we will but "come unto Him." There certainly can and will be plenty of external difficulties in life; nevertheless, the soul that comes unto Christ dwells within a personal fortress, a veritable palace of perfect peace. "Whoso hearkeneth unto me," Jehovah says, "shall dwell safely, and shall be quiet from fear of evil" (Prov. 1:33).

That is exactly what Paul said to the Corinthians. Trying to help them keep their chin up—and the Corinthians had a lot to be grim about—he wrote: "Blessed be God, even the Father of our Lord Jesus Christ, the Father of mercies, and the God of all comfort; who comforteth us in all our tribulation, that we may be able to comfort them which are in any trouble, by the comfort wherewith we ourselves are comforted of God" (2 Cor. 1:3–4).

Jesus taught the same thing to the Nephites, who also lived in a difficult world. "For the mountains shall depart and the hills be removed," He said, "but my kindness shall not depart from thee, neither shall the covenant of my peace be removed [from thee]" (3 Ne. 22:10; see vv. 13–14). I love that. The hills and the mountains may disappear. The seas and oceans may dry up completely. The least likely things in the world may happen, but "my kindness shall not depart from thee, neither shall the covenant of my peace be removed [from thee]." After all, He has, He reminds us, "graven thee upon the palms of my hands" (1 Ne. 21:16). Considering the incomprehensible cost of the Crucifixion, Christ is not going to turn His back on us now.

The Lord has probably spoken enough such comforting words to supply the whole universe, it would seem, and yet we see all around us unhappy Latter-day Saints, worried Latter-day Saints, and gloomy Latter-day Saints into whose troubled hearts not one of these innumerable consoling words seems to be allowed to enter. In fact, I think some of us must have that remnant of Puritan heritage still with us that says it is somehow wrong to be comforted or helped, that we are supposed to be miserable about something.

Consider, for example, the Savior's benediction upon His disciples even as He moved toward the pain and agony of Gethsemane and Calvary. On that very night, the night of the greatest suffering that has ever taken place in the world or that ever will take place, the Savior said, "Peace I leave with you, my peace I give unto you. . . . Let not your heart be troubled, neither let it be afraid" (John 14:27).

I submit to you, that may be one of the Savior's commandments that is, even in the hearts of otherwise faithful Latter-day Saints, almost universally disobeyed; and yet I wonder whether our resistance to this invitation could be any more grievous to the Lord's merciful heart. I can tell you this as a parent: as concerned as I would be if somewhere in their lives one of my children were seriously troubled or unhappy or disobedient, nevertheless I would be infinitely more devastated if I felt that at such a time that child could not trust me to help or thought his or her interest was unimportant to me or unsafe in my care. In that same spirit, I am convinced that none of us can appreciate how deeply it wounds the loving heart of the Savior of the world when He finds that His people do not feel confident in His care or secure in His hands or trust in His commandments.

Just because God is God, just because Christ is Christ, they cannot do other than care for us and bless us and help us if we will but come unto them, approaching their throne of grace in meekness and lowliness of heart. They can't help but bless us. They have to. It is their nature. That is why Joseph Smith gave those lectures on faith, so we would understand the nature of godliness and in the process have enough confidence to come unto Christ and find peace to our souls. There is not a single loophole or curveball or open trench to fall into for the man or woman who walks the path that Christ walks. When He says, "Come, follow me" (Luke 18:22), He means that He knows where the quicksand is and where the thorns are and the best way to handle the slippery slope near the summit of our personal mountains. He knows it all, and He knows the way. He is the way.

Once we have come unto Christ and found the miracle of His "covenant of peace," I think we are under obligation to help others do so, just as Paul said in that verse to the Corinthians—to live as much like He lived as we possibly can and to do as much of what He did in order that others may walk in this same peace and have this same reassurance.

Much of the comfort I am speaking of comes from the Savior's power to heal—to heal the wounds of life or of sorrow or, where necessary, of transgression. I would ask you now to help with this healing, healing for others, healing for those you love and, yes, perhaps especially for those you don't. The people around us need a lot of help, and I think the Lord expects us to join in that effort. I think that is what He meant when He said, in essence, Come, see what I do, and watch how I spend my time.

Following my call to the Quorum of the Twelve, I read all of the standard works again, with special concentration on anything said or done by the Savior. Inasmuch as I couldn't sleep, I seemed to have more than the usual amount of time and privacy to consider these great teachings. As I put somewhat new and often tear-filled eyes to the scriptures, I saw perhaps for the first time the majesty of Christ's healing influence—probably because I was needing so much of that myself.

Most of the healing I am speaking of is not necessarily that of administering to the physically sick, though we surely should be ready and worthy to either request or give such a blessing at a moment's notice according to the order of the priesthood. No, what I refer to are those rending, wrenching illnesses of the soul that need to be healed but may be quite personal—some burden held deep inside, some weariness that is not always particularly obvious to the rest of the world. Here in the shadow of the twenty-first century we are likely to face slightly more meta-physical sicknesses than those biblical ills of old, such as leprosy and consumption.

On the example of the Savior Himself and His call to His Apostles, and with the need for peace and comfort ringing in our ears, I ask you to be a healer, be a helper, be someone who joins in the work of Christ in lifting burdens, in making the load lighter, in making things better. As children, when we had a bump or a bruise, didn't we say to Mom or Dad, "Make it better"? Well, lots of people on your right hand and on your left are carrying bumps and bruises that they hope will be healed and made whole. Someone you know is carrying a spiritual or physical or emotional burden of some sort, or some other affliction drawn from life's catalog of a thousand kinds of sorrow. In the spirit of Christ's first invitation to His twelve Apostles, jump into this work. Help people. Heal old wounds and try to make things better.

Often we can, usually unwittingly, be quite insensitive to the circumstances and difficulties of those around us. We all have problems, and ultimately each individual has to take responsibility for his or her own happiness. None of us is so free of difficulty ourselves or so endowed with time and money that we can do nothing but tend "the wounded and the weary."[3] Nevertheless, in looking to the Savior's life for an example, I suspect we can probably find a way to do more of that than we do.

Since I have mentioned repentance, let me repent a bit myself—or at least do the confessing part and hope even now there is a way for me to make some restitution.

My confession is that I wish I could go back to my youth and there have another chance to reach out to those who, at the time, didn't fall very solidly onto my radar scope. Youth want to feel included and important, to have the feeling they matter to others. Young people deserve to have true friendships—the real value of which, like our health, may never be realized until we face life without them. I think that my problem was not that I had too few friends but almost too many. But it is the associations I didn't have, the friends I didn't reach, that cause me some pain now all these years later.

Let me cite just one case, which will be guilt enough for now. In 1979 we held in St. George, Utah, our twenty-year class reunion for Dixie High School. We had great high school years filled with state football and basketball championships and a host of other "hometown, USA" memories. An effort was made to find current addresses for the entire class and get everyone to the reunion.

In the midst of all that fun, I remember the terribly painful letter written by one very bright—but, in her childhood, somewhat less popular—young woman who wrote something like this:

"Congratulations to all of us for having survived long enough to have a twenty-year class reunion. I hope everyone has a wonderful time. But don't reserve a place for me. I have, in fact, spent most of those twenty years trying to forget the painful moments of our school days together. Now that I am nearly over those feelings of loneliness and shattered self-esteem, I cannot bring myself to see all of the class and run the risk of remembering all of that again. Have a good time and forgive me. It is my problem, not yours. Maybe I can come at the thirty-year mark."

Which, I am very happy to report, she did. But she was terribly wrong about one thing—it was our problem, and we knew it.

71

I have wept for her—my friend—and other friends like her in my youth for whom I and a lot of others obviously were not masters of "the healer's art."[4] We simply were not the Savior's agents or disciples that He intends people to be. I cannot help but wonder what I might have done to watch out a little more for the ones not included, to make sure the gesture of a friendly word or a listening ear or a little low-cost casual talk and shared time might have reached far enough to include those hanging on the outer edge of the social circle, and in some cases barely hanging on at all.

Jesus said in His most remarkable sermon ever: "For if ye love them which love you, what reward have ye? do not even the publicans the same? And if ye salute your brethren only, what do ye more than others? do not even the publicans so?" (Matt. 5:46–47).

I make an appeal for us to reach beyond our own contentment, to move out of our own comfort and companion zones, to reach those who may not always be so easy to reach.

If we do less, what distinguishes us from the biblical publican? I might not have been able to heal all the wounds of those I met in my young adult years, but I can't help thinking that if I had tried even harder to be more of a healer, more of a helper, a little less focused on myself and a little more centered on others, some days in the lives of those God placed in my path would have been much better. "I have called you friends," the Savior said in one of His highest compliments to His disciples (John 15:15). Therefore, "love one another, as I have loved you" (John 15:12).

One last piece of counsel regarding coming to Christ; it comes from an unusual incident in the life of the Savior that holds a lesson for us all. It was after Jesus had performed the miracle of feeding the 5,000 from five loaves of bread and two fishes. (By the way, let me pause here to say, Don't worry about Christ running out of ability to help you. His grace is sufficient. That is the spiritual, eternal lesson of the feeding of the 5,000.) After Jesus had fed the multitude, He sent them away and put His disciples into a fishing boat to cross over to the other side of the Sea of Galilee. He then "went up into a mountain apart to pray" (Matt. 14:23).

We aren't told all of the circumstances of the disciples as they set out in their boat, but it was toward evening, and certainly it was a stormy night. The winds must have been ferocious from the start. Because of the winds, these men probably never even raised the sails but labored only with the oars—and labor it would have been. We know this because by the time of "the fourth watch of the night" (Matt. 14:25)—that is somewhere between three and six in the morning—they had gone only a few miles. By then the ship was caught up in a truly violent storm, a storm like those that can still sweep down on the Sea of Galilee to this day.

But, as always, Christ was watching over them. He always does, remember? Seeing their difficulty, the Savior simply took the most direct approach to their boat, striding out across the waves to help them, walking on the water as surely as He had walked upon the land. In their moment of great extremity, the disciples looked and saw in the darkness this wonder in a fluttering robe coming toward them on the ridges of the sea. They cried out in terror at the sight, thinking that it was a phantom upon the waves. Then, through the storm and darkness—when the sea seems so great and little boats seem so small—there came the ultimate and reassuring voice of peace from their Master. "It is I," He said; "be not afraid" (Matt. 14:27).

This scriptural account reminds us that the first step in coming to Christ, or in His coming to us, may fill us with something very much like sheer terror. It shouldn't, but it sometimes does. One of the grand ironies of the gospel is that the very source of help and safety being offered us is the thing from which we may, in our mortal shortsightedness, flee. For whatever the reason, I have seen investigators run from baptism, I have seen elders run from a mission call, I have seen sweethearts run from marriage, and I have seen members run from challenging callings. Too often too many of us run from the very things that will bless us and save us and soothe us. Too often we see gospel commitments and commandments as something to be feared and forsaken.

Let me quote the marvelous Elder James E. Talmage of the Quorum of the Twelve Apostles on this matter: "Into every adult human life come experiences like unto the battling of the storm-tossed voyagers with contrary winds and threatening seas; ofttimes the night of struggle and danger is far advanced before succor appears; and then, too frequently the saving aid is mistaken for a greater terror. [But,] as came unto [these disciples] in the midst of the turbulent waters, so comes to all who toil in faith, the voice of the Deliverer—'It is I; be not afraid.'"[5]

Elder Talmage used the word *succor*. Do you know its meaning? It is used often in the scriptures to describe Christ's care for and attention to us. It means literally "to run to." What a magnificent way to describe the Savior's urgent effort in our behalf! Even as He calls us to come to Him and follow Him, He is unfailingly running to help us.

Finally recognizing the Master that night, Peter exclaimed,

"Lord, if it be thou, bid me come unto thee on the water" (Matt. 14:28).

And Christ's answer to him was as it always is to all of us: "Come," He said (Matt. 14:29).

Instantly, as was his nature, Peter sprang over the vessel's side and into the troubled waves. While his eyes were fixed upon the Lord, the wind could toss his hair and the spray could drench his robes, but all was well—he was coming to Christ. Only when his faith and his focus wavered, only when he removed his glance from the Master to see the furious waves and the black gulf beneath him, only then did he begin to sink. In fear he cried out, "Lord, save me" (Matt. 14:29–30).

In some disappointment, the "Master of ocean and earth and skies"[6] stretched out His hand and grasped the drowning disciple with the gentle rebuke, "O thou of little faith, where-fore didst thou doubt?" (Matt. 14:31).[7]

Jesus is the Christ, the Son of the living God. This is His true and living Church. He wishes us to come unto Him, to fol-low Him, to be comforted by Him. Then He wishes us to give comfort to others. However halting our steps are toward Him—though they shouldn't be halting at all—His steps are never halting toward us. May we have enough faith to accept the goodness of God and the mercy of His Only Begotten Son. May we come unto Him and His gospel and be healed. And may we do more to heal others in the process. When the storms of life make this difficult, may we still follow His bidding to "come," keeping our eye fixed on Him forever and single to His glory. In doing so, we too will walk triumphantly over the swelling waves of life's difficulties and remain unterrified amid any rising winds of despair.

Notes

From a talk given at a Church Educational System Young Adult fireside at Brigham Young University, 2 March 1997.

1. Joseph Smith, *Lectures on Faith* (Salt Lake City: Deseret Book, 1985), 41–42.

2. Smith, *Lectures on Faith*, 42.

3. Susan Evans McCloud, "Lord, I Would Follow Thee," in *Hymns of The Church of Jesus Christ of Latter-day Saints* (Salt Lake City: The Church of Jesus Christ of Latter-day Saints, 1985), no. 220.

4. Ibid.

5. James E. Talmage, *Jesus the Christ* (Salt Lake City: Deseret News, 1916), 337.

6. Mary Ann Baker, "Master, the Tempest Is Raging," in *Hymns,* no. 105.

7. See Frederic W. Farrar, *The Life of Christ* (Salt Lake City: Bookcraft, 1994), 310–13.

7

"HE LOVED THEM UNTO THE END"

Ⓘt is no small thing to "sustain" another person. The word literally means to "uphold" or, if you prefer, to "hold up." When we sustain life, we nourish it, we keep it going. When we sustain a friend or a neighbor or a stranger in the street, we give support, we share strength, we provide help. We hold each other up under the weight of present circumstance. We bear one another's burdens under the heavy personal pressures of life.

As with all else in our experience, the Lord Jesus Christ is our exemplar and ideal in this very important matter of providing sustenance. His is the ultimate arm of strength and His the endurance which endures all things. At no time did He demonstrate that unfailing devotion more clearly than during the final moments of His earthly life, hours when He might well have wished that others could have been sustaining Him.

As the sacred supper of that ultimate Passover was being prepared, Jesus was under the strain of deep and profound emotion. Only He knew what lay immediately ahead, but perhaps even He did not fully anticipate the depth of pain to which He must go before it could be said, "The Son of Man hath descended below them all" (D&C 122:8).

In the midst of this meal and such thoughts, Christ quietly arose, girded Himself as a slave or servant would, and knelt to wash the Apostles' feet (see John 13:4–17). This small circle of believers in this scarcely founded kingdom were about to pass through their severest trial, so He would set aside His own increasing anguish in order that He might yet once more serve and strengthen them. It does not matter that no one washed His feet. In transcendent humility, He would continue to teach and to cleanse them. He would to the final hour—and beyond—be their sustaining servant. As John wrote, who was there and watched the wonder of it all, "Having loved his own which were in the world, he loved them unto the end" (John 13:1).

So it had been, and so it was to be—through the night, and through the pain, and forever. He would always be their strength, and no anguish in His own soul would ever keep Him from that sustaining role.

In the moonlit silence of that Near Eastern night, every acute pain, every heartfelt grief, every crushing wrong and human hurt experienced by every man, woman, and child in the human family was to be heaped upon His weary shoulders. But in such a moment, when someone might have said it to Him, He rather says to us, "Let not your heart be troubled, neither let it be afraid" (John 14:27).

"Ye shall be sorrowful," He said—sad, lonely, frightened, and sometimes even persecuted—"but your sorrow shall be turned into joy. . . . Be of good cheer; I have overcome the world" (John 16:20, 33).

How can He speak that way? Of good cheer and joy? On a night like this? With the pain He knew was just ahead? But those are the blessings He always brought, and that is how He always spoke—to the very end.

We cannot know to what extent His disciples fully understood the approaching events, but we do know that Christ faced His final moments alone. In one of the truly candid comments He would make to His brethren, He said, "My soul is exceeding sorrowful, even unto death" (Matt. 26:38). And He left them to do what only He could do. The Light of the World stepped away from human company and entered the garden grove to wrestle with the prince of darkness alone. Moving forward, kneeling, falling forward on His face, He cried with an anguish you and I will never know, "O my Father, if it be possible, let this cup pass from me" (Matt. 26:39). But He knew, for our sakes, that it could not pass and that He must drink that bitter cup to the dregs!

His disciples, understandably, were weary and soon fell asleep. What of Christ's sleep? What of His fatigue? What rest or slumber will sustain Him through such an agonizing ordeal? That is simply not His concern here, nor does it ever seem to be. He will endure. He will triumph. He will not falter nor fail us.

Even in crucifixion He would reign with the benevolence and bearing of a King. Of those who rend His flesh and spill His blood He says, "Father, forgive them; for they know not what they do" (Luke 23:34). And to the penitent thief at His side He gently promises paradise. To His beloved mother He is unable to make any caring gesture with His hands. So He simply looks at her and says, "Woman, behold thy son!" Then commending to John her future care, He declares, "Behold thy mother!" (John 19:26–27). He would be concerned for others—but especially for her—to the very end.

Because He must ultimately tread this winepress of redemption unaided, can He endure the darkest moment of them all, the shock of the greatest pain? This comes not with thorns and with nails, but with the terror of feeling utterly alone: "Eloi, Eloi, lama sabachthani? . . . My God, my God, why hast thou forsaken me?" (Mark 15:34). Can He bear all of our sins and our fear and loneliness too? He did and He does and He will.

We do not know how such great sorrow can be borne, but it is no wonder the sun hid its face in shame. No wonder the veil of the temple was rent. No wonder the very earth convulsed at the plight of this perfect child. And at least one Roman centurion who saw all of this sensed something of what it had meant. In awe, he uttered the declaration for all eternity, "Truly this was the Son of God" (Matt. 27:54).

Life has its share of some fear and some failure. Sometimes things fall short, don't quite measure up. Sometimes in both personal and public life, we are seemingly left without strength to go on. Sometimes people fail us, or economies and circumstance fail us, and life with its hardship and heartache can leave us feeling very alone.

But when such difficult moments come to us, I testify that there is one thing which will never, ever fail us. One thing alone will stand the test of all time, of all tribulation, all trouble, and all transgression. One thing only never faileth—and that is the pure love of Christ.

"I remember," Moroni cries to the Savior of the world, "that thou hast said that thou hast loved the world, even unto the laying down of thy life for the world. . . .

". . . Now I know," he writes, "that this love which thou hast had for the children of men is charity" (Ether 12:33–34).

Having watched a dispensation die and an entire civilization destroy itself, Moroni quotes his father for any who will listen in some later ("latter") day, "If ye have not charity, ye are nothing" (Moro. 7:46). Only the pure love of Christ will see us through. It is Christ's love which suffereth long and is kind. It is Christ's love which is not puffed up nor easily provoked. Only His pure love enables Him—and us—to bear all things, believe all things, hope all things, and endure all things (see Moro. 7:45).

> *Oh, love effulgent, love divine!*
> *What debt of gratitude is mine,*
> *That in his off'ring I have part*
> *And hold a place within his heart.*[1]

I testify that having loved us who are in the world, Christ loves us to the end. His pure love never fails us. Not now. Not ever. Not ever. Of that divine sustaining vote for all of us, I testify.

Notes

From a talk given at general conference, September 1989.

1. Edward P. Kimball, "God Loved Us, So He Sent His Son," in *Hymns of The Church of Jesus Christ of Latter-day Saints* (Salt Lake City: The Church of Jesus Christ of Latter-day Saints, 1985), no. 187.

8

"The Peaceable Things of the Kingdom"

The great Isaiah foresaw the restoration of the gospel and establishment of the Church "in the top of the mountains":

"And it shall come to pass in the last days, that the mountain of the Lord's house shall be established in the top of the mountains, and shall be exalted above the hills; and all nations shall flow unto it.

"And many people shall go and say, Come ye, and let us go up to the mountain of the Lord, to the house of the God of Jacob; and he will teach us of his ways, and we will walk in his paths: for out of Zion shall go forth the law, and the word of the Lord from Jerusalem" (Isa. 2:2–3).

Of such comforting latter-day direction, including its divine source, Isaiah would go on to say: "How beautiful upon the mountains are the feet of him that bringeth good tidings, that publisheth peace" (Isa. 52:7).

Peace and good tidings; good tidings and peace. These are among the ultimate blessings that the gospel of Jesus Christ brings a troubled world and the troubled people who live in it, solutions to personal struggles and human sinfulness, a source of strength for days of weariness and hours of genuine despair. The Church of Jesus Christ of Latter-day Saints declares that it is the Only Begotten Son of God Himself who gives us this help and this hope. Such assurance is as "firm as the mountains around us."[1] As the Book of Mormon prophet Abinadi made clear in a slight variation of Isaiah's exclamation:

"O how beautiful upon the mountains are the feet of him that bringeth good tidings, that *is the founder of peace*, yea, even the Lord, who has redeemed his people; yea, him who has granted salvation unto his people" (Mosiah 15:18; emphasis added).

Ultimately it is Christ who is beautiful upon the mountain. And it is His merciful promise of "peace in this world," His good tidings of "eternal life in the world to come" (D&C 59:23), that make us fall at His feet and call His name blessed and give thanks for the restoration of His true and living Church.

The search for peace is one of the ultimate quests of the human soul. We all have highs and lows, but such times come and they usually always go. Kind neighbors assist. Beautiful sunshine brings encouragement. A good night's sleep usually works wonders. But there are times in all of our lives when deep sorrow or suffering or fear or loneliness makes us cry out for the peace which only God Himself can bring. These are times of piercing spiritual hunger when even the dearest friends cannot fully come to our aid.

Perhaps you know people in your local ward or stake—or in your own home—courageous people who are carrying heavy burdens and feeling private pain, who are walking through the dark valleys of this world's tribulation. Some may be desperately worried about a husband or a wife or a child, worried about their health or their happiness or their faithfulness in keeping the commandments. Some are living with physical pain, or emotional pain, or disabilities that come with age. Some are troubled as to how to make ends meet financially, and some ache with the private loneliness of an empty house or an empty room or simply empty arms.

These beloved people seek the Lord and His word with particular urgency, often revealing their true emotions only when the scriptures are opened or when the hymns are sung or when the prayers are offered. Sometimes only then do the rest of us realize they feel near the end of their strength—they are tired in brain and body and heart, they wonder if they can get through another week or another day or sometimes just another hour. They are desperate for the Lord's help, and they know that in such times of extremity nothing else will do.

Well, at least one of the purposes of the Church and the teachings of the prophets down through the ages is to declare to these very people that the Lord is equally fervent in trying to reach them, that when there is trouble His hopes and His striving and His efforts greatly exceed our own and his aid never ceases.

We have been promised, "He that keepeth [us] will not slumber, . . . nor [will he] sleep" (Ps. 121:3–4).

Christ and His angels and His prophets forever labor to buoy up our spirits, steady our nerves, calm our hearts, and send us forth with renewed strength and resolute hope. They wish all to know that "if God be for us, who can be against us?" (Rom. 8:31). In the world we shall have tribulation, but we are to be of good cheer. Christ has overcome the world (see John 16:33).

85

Through His suffering and His obedience, He has earned and rightly bears the crown of "Prince of Peace" (Isa. 9:6; 2 Ne. 19:6).

In that spirit, we declare to all the world that for real and abiding peace to come we must strive to be more like that exemplary Son of God. Many among us are trying to do that. We salute you for your obedience, your forbearance, your waiting faithfully upon the Lord for the strength you seek which will surely come. Some of us, on the other hand, need to make some changes, need to make greater effort in gospel living. And change we can. The very beauty of the word *repentance* is the promise of escaping old problems and old habits and old sorrows and old sins. It is among the most hopeful and encouraging— and yes, most peaceful—words in the gospel vocabulary. In seeking true peace, some of us need to improve what has to be improved, confess what needs to be confessed, forgive what has to be forgiven, and forget what should be forgotten in order that serenity can come to us. If there is a commandment we are breaking, and as a result it is breaking us and hurting those who love us, let us call down the power of the Lord Jesus Christ to help us, to free us, to lead us through repentance to that peace "which passeth all understanding" (Philip. 4:7).

And when God has forgiven us, which He is so eternally anxious to do, may we have the good sense to walk away from those problems, to leave them alone, to let the past bury the past. If one of you has made a mistake, even a serious mistake, but you have done all you can according to the teachings of the Lord and the governance of the Church to confess it and feel sorrow for it and set it as right as can be, then trust in God, walk into His light, and leave those ashes behind you. Someone once said that repentance is the first pressure we feel when drawn to

the bosom of God. For real peace may I recommend an immediate rush to the bosom of God, leaving behind you all that
would bring sorrow to your soul or heartache to those who love
you. "Depart from evil," the scripture says, "and do good" (Ps.
34:14).

Closely related to our own obligation to repent is the generosity of letting others do the same—we are to forgive even as
we are forgiven. In this we participate in the very essence of the
Atonement of Jesus Christ. Surely the most majestic moment
of that fateful Friday, when nature convulsed and the veil of the
temple was rent, was that unspeakably merciful moment when
Christ said, "Father, forgive them; for they know not what they
do" (Luke 23:34). As our advocate with the Father, He is still
making that same plea today—in your behalf and in mine.

Here, as in all things, Jesus set the standard for us to follow.
Life is too short to be spent nursing animosities or keeping a box
score of offenses against us—you know, no runs, no hits, all
errors. We don't want God to remember our sins, so there is
something fundamentally wrong in our relentlessly trying to
remember those of others.

When we have been hurt, undoubtedly God takes into
account what wrongs were done to us and what provocations
there are for our resentments, but clearly the more provocation
there is and the more excuse we can find for our hurt, all the
more reason for us to forgive and be delivered from the destructive hell of such poisonous venom and anger.[2] It is one of those
ironies of godhood that in order to find peace, the offended as
well as the offender must engage the principle of forgiveness.

Yes, peace is a very precious commodity, a truly heartfelt
need, and there are many things we can do to achieve it. But—
for whatever reason—life has its moments when uninterrupted

peace may seem to elude us for a season. We may wonder why there are such times in life, particularly when we may be trying harder than we have ever tried to live worthy of God's blessings and obtain His help. When problems or sorrows or sadness come and they *don't* seem to be our fault, what are we to make of their unwelcome appearance?

With time and perspective we recognize that such problems in life do come for a purpose, if only to allow the one who faces such despair to be convinced that he really does need divine strength beyond himself, that she really does need the offer of heaven's hand. Those who feel no need for mercy usually never seek it and almost never bestow it. Those who have never had a heartache or a weakness or felt lonely or forsaken never have had to cry unto heaven for relief of such personal pain. Surely it is better to find the goodness of God and the grace of Christ, even at the price of despair, than to risk living our lives in a moral or material complacency that has never felt any need for faith or forgiveness, any need for redemption or relief.

A life without problems or limitations or challenges—life without "opposition in all things," as Lehi phrased it (2 Ne. 2:11)—would paradoxically but in very fact be less rewarding and less ennobling than one which confronts—even frequently confronts—difficulty and disappointment and sorrow. As beloved Eve said, were it not for the difficulties faced in a fallen world, neither she nor Adam nor any of the rest of us ever would have known "the joy of our redemption, and the eternal life which God giveth unto all the obedient" (Moses 5:11).

So life has its oppositions and its conflicts, and the gospel of Jesus Christ has answers and assurances. In a time of terrible civil warfare, one of the most gifted leaders ever to strive to hold a nation together said what could be said of marriages and families and friendships. Praying for peace, pleading for peace, seeking peace in any way that would not compromise union, Abraham Lincoln said in those dark, dark days of his first inaugural address: "Though passion may have strained, it must not break our bonds of affection. The mystic chords of memory," he said, "will yet swell . . . when again touched, as surely they will be, by the better angels of our nature."[3]

"The better angels of our nature." That is much of what the Church and the gospel of Jesus Christ are about: the appeal today and tomorrow and forever to be better, to be cleaner, to be kinder, to be holier, to seek peace and always be believing.

I have personally known in my own life the realization of the promise "that the everlasting God, . . . the Creator of the ends of the earth, fainteth not, neither is [he] weary." I am a witness that "he giveth power to the faint; and to them that have no might he increaseth strength" (Isa. 40:28–29).

I know that in times of fear or fatigue, "they that wait upon the Lord shall renew their strength; they shall mount up with wings as eagles; they shall run, and not be weary; and they shall walk, and not faint" (Isa. 40:31).

We receive the gift of such majestic might and sanctifying renewal through the redeeming grace of the Lord Jesus Christ. He has overcome the world, and if we will take upon us His name and "walk in his paths" (Isa. 2:3) and keep our covenants with Him, we shall, ere long, have peace. Such a reward is not only possible; it is certain.

"For the mountains shall depart and the hills be removed, but my kindness shall not depart from thee, neither shall the covenant of my peace be removed, saith the Lord that hath mercy on thee" (3 Ne. 22:10).

Of Him and His good tidings, of the publication of His

peace in this His true Church, and of His living prophet, I bear grateful and joyful witness.

Notes

From a talk given at general conference, October 1996.

1. Ruth May Fox, "Carry On," in *Hymns of The Church of Jesus Christ of Latter-day Saints* (Salt Lake City: The Church of Jesus Christ of Latter-day Saints, 1985), no. 255.

2. Adapted from George Macdonald, in *George MacDonald, An Anthology*, C. S. Lewis, editor (New York: Macmillan Publishing Co., Inc., 1947), 6–7.

3. Abraham Lincoln, First Inaugural Address, 4 March 1861, in *Speeches of Abraham Lincoln* (New York: Lincoln Centenary Association, 1908), 319.

9

"AN HIGH PRIEST OF GOOD THINGS TO COME"

On those days when we have special need of heaven's help, we would do well to remember one of the titles given to the Savior in the epistle to the Hebrews. Speaking of Jesus' "more excellent ministry" and why He "is the mediator of a better covenant" filled with "better promises," this author—presumably the Apostle Paul—tells us that through His mediation and atonement, Christ became "an high priest of good things to come" (Heb. 8:6; 9:11).

Every one of us has times when we need to know things will get better. Moroni spoke of it in the Book of Mormon as "hope for a better world" (Ether 12:4). For emotional health and spiritual stamina, everyone needs to be able to look forward to some respite, to something pleasant and renewing and hopeful, whether that blessing be near at hand or still some distance ahead. It is enough just to know we can get there, that however

91

measured or far away, there is the promise of "good things to come."

My declaration is that this is precisely what the gospel of Jesus Christ offers us, especially in times of need. There *is* help. There *is* happiness. There really *is* light at the end of the tunnel. It is the Light of the World, the Bright and Morning Star, the "light that is endless, that can never be darkened" (Mosiah 16:9; see John 8:12; Rev. 22:16). It is the very Son of God Himself. In loving praise far beyond Romeo's reach, we say, "What light through yonder window breaks?" It is the return of hope, and Jesus is the Sun.[1] To any who may be struggling to see that light and find that hope, I say: Hold on. Keep trying. God loves you. Things will improve. Christ comes to you in His "more excellent ministry" with a future of "better promises." He is your "high priest of good things to come."

I think of newly called missionaries leaving family and friends to face, on occasion, some rejection and some discouragement and, at least in the beginning, a moment or two of homesickness and perhaps a little fear.

I think of young mothers and fathers who are faithfully having their families while still in school—or just newly out—trying to make ends meet even as they hope for a brighter financial future someday. At the same time, I think of other parents who would give any earthly possession they own to have a wayward child return.

I think of single parents who face all of this but face it alone, having confronted death or divorce, alienation or abandonment, or some other misfortune they had not foreseen in happier days and certainly had not wanted.

I think of those who want to be married and aren't, those who desire to have children and cannot, those who have

92

acquaintances but very few friends, those who are grieving over the death of a loved one or are themselves ill with disease. I think of those who suffer from sin—their own or someone else's—who need to know there is a way back and that happiness can be restored. I think of the disconsolate and downtrodden who feel life has passed them by, or now wish that it would pass them by. To all of these and so many more, I say: Cling to your faith. Hold on to your hope. "Pray always, and be believing" (D&C 90:24). Indeed, as Paul wrote of Abraham, he "against [all] hope believed in hope" and "staggered not . . . through unbelief." He "was strong in faith" and was "fully persuaded that, what [God] had promised, he was able . . . to perform" (Rom. 4:18, 20–21).

Even if you cannot always see that silver lining on your clouds, God can, for He is the very source of the light you seek. He does love you, and He knows your fears. He hears your prayers. He is your Heavenly Father, and surely He matches with His own the tears His children shed.

In spite of this counsel, I know some of you do truly feel at sea, in the most frightening sense of that term. Out in troubled waters, you may even now be crying with the poet:

> *It darkens. I have lost the ford.*
> *There is a change on all things made.*
> *The rocks have evil faces, Lord,*
> *And I am [sore] afraid.* [2]

No, it is not without a recognition of life's tempests but fully and directly because of them that I testify of God's love and the Savior's power to calm the storm. Always remember in that biblical story that He was out there on the water also, that He faced the worst of it right along with the newest and youngest

and most fearful. Only One who has fought against those omi-
nous waves is justified in telling us—*as well as the sea*—to "be
still" (Mark 4:39; D&C 101:16). Only One who has taken the
full brunt of such adversity could ever be justified in telling us
in such times to "be of good cheer" (John 16:33; D&C 68:6).
Such counsel is not a jaunty pep talk about the power of positive thinking, though positive thinking is much needed in the
world. No, Christ knows better than all others that the trials of
life can be very deep, and we are not shallow people if we
struggle with them. But even as the Lord avoids sugary rheto-
ric, He rebukes faithlessness, and He deplores pessimism. He
expects us to believe!

No one's eyes were more penetrating than His, and much of
what He saw pierced His heart. Surely His ears heard every cry
of distress, every sound of want and despair. To a degree far more
than we will ever understand, He was "a man of sorrows, and
acquainted with grief" (Isa. 53:3; Mosiah 14:3). Indeed, to the
layman in the streets of Judea, Christ's career must have seemed
a failure, a tragedy, a good man totally overwhelmed by the evils
surrounding Him and the misdeeds of others. He was misunder-
stood or misrepresented, even hated from the beginning. No
matter what He said or did, His statements were twisted,
His actions suspected, His motives impugned. In the entire
history of the world no one has ever loved so purely or served
so selflessly—and been treated so diabolically for His effort. Yet
nothing could break His faith in His Father's plan or His
Father's promises. Even in those darkest hours at Gethsemane
and Calvary, He pressed on, continuing to trust in the very God
whom He momentarily feared had forsaken Him.

Because Christ's eyes were unfailingly fixed on the future,
He could endure all that was required of Him, suffer as no man

can suffer except it be "unto death," as King Benjamin said (Mosiah 3:7), look upon the wreckage of individual lives and the promises of ancient Israel lying in ruins around Him and still say then and now, "Let not your heart be troubled, neither let it be afraid" (John 14:27). How could He do this? How could He believe it? *Because He knows that for the faithful, things will be made right soon enough. He is a King; He speaks for the crown; He knows what can be promised.* He knows that "the Lord . . . will be a refuge for the oppressed, a refuge in times of trouble. . . . For the needy shall not alway[s] be forgotten: the expectation of the poor shall not perish for ever" (Ps. 9:9, 18). He knows that "the Lord is nigh unto them that are of a broken heart; and saveth such as be of a contrite spirit." He knows that "the Lord redeemeth the soul of his servants: and none of them that trust in him shall be desolate" (Ps. 34:18, 22).

Forgive me for a personal conclusion, which does not represent the terrible burdens so many of you carry, but it *is* meant to be encouraging. Thirty years ago last month, a little family set out to cross the United States to attend graduate school—no money, an old car, every earthly possession they owned packed into less than half the space of the smallest U-Haul trailer available. Bidding their apprehensive parents farewell, they drove exactly thirty-four miles up the highway, at which point their beleaguered car erupted.

Pulling off the freeway onto a frontage road, the young father surveyed the steam, matched it with his own, then left his trusting wife and two innocent children—the youngest just three months old—to wait in the car while he walked the three miles or so to the southern Utah metropolis of Kanarraville, population then, I suppose, sixty-five. Some water was secured at the edge of town, and a very kind citizen offered a drive back

95

to the stranded family. The car was attended to and slowly—
very slowly—driven back to St. George for inspection—U-Haul
trailer and all.

After more than two hours of checking and rechecking, no
immediate problem could be detected, so once again the journey was begun. In exactly the same amount of elapsed time at
exactly the same location on that highway with exactly the
same pyrotechnics from under the hood, the car exploded again.
It could not have been fifteen feet from the earlier collapse,
probably not five feet from it! Obviously the most precise laws
of automotive physics were at work.

Now feeling more foolish than angry, the chagrined young
father once more left his trusting loved ones and started the
long walk for help once again. This time the man providing the
water said, "Either you or that fellow who looks just like you
ought to get a new radiator for that car." For the second time a
kind neighbor offered a lift back to the same automobile and its
anxious little occupants. He didn't know whether to laugh or to
cry at the plight of this young family.

"How far have you come?" he said. "Thirty-four miles," I
answered. "How much farther do you have to go?" "Twenty-six
hundred miles," I said. "Well, *you* might make that trip, and
your wife and those two little kiddies might make that trip, but
none of you are going to make it in *that* car." He proved to be
prophetic on all counts.

Just two weeks ago this weekend, I drove by that exact spot
where the freeway turnoff leads to a frontage road, just three
miles or so west of Kanarraville, Utah. That same beautiful and
loyal wife, my dearest friend and greatest supporter for all these
years, was curled up asleep in the seat beside me. The two
children in the story, and the little brother who later joined

them, have long since grown up and served missions, married perfectly, and are now raising children of their own. The automobile we were driving this time was modest but very pleasant and very safe. In fact, except for me and my lovely Pat situated so peacefully at my side, nothing of that moment two weeks ago was even remotely like the distressing circumstances of three decades earlier.

Yet in my mind's eye, for just an instant, I thought perhaps I saw on that side road an old car with a devoted young wife and two little children making the best of a bad situation there. Just ahead of them I imagined that I saw a young fellow walking toward Kanarraville, with plenty of distance still ahead of him. His shoulders seemed to be slumping a little, the weight of a young father's fear evident in his pace. In the scriptural phrase, his hands did seem to "hang down" (D&C 81:5). In that imaginary instant, I couldn't help calling out to him: "Don't give up, boy. Don't you quit. You keep walking. You keep trying. There is help and happiness ahead—a lot of it—thirty years of it now, and still counting. You keep your chin up. It will be all right in the end. Trust God and believe in good things to come."

I testify that God lives, that He is our Eternal Father, that He loves each of us with a love divine. I testify that Jesus Christ is His Only Begotten Son in the flesh and, having triumphed in this world, is an heir of eternity, a joint-heir with God, and now stands on the right hand of His Father. I testify that this is Their true Church and that They sustain us in our hour of need—and always will, even if we cannot recognize that intervention. Some blessings come soon, some come late, and some don't come until heaven; but for those who embrace the gospel of Jesus Christ, *they come*. Of that I personally attest.

Notes

From a talk given at general conference, October 1999.

1. William Shakespeare, *Romeo and Juliet*, act 2, scene 2, lines 2–3; see Malachi 4:2.

2. Joseph Hilaire Belloc, "The Prophet Lost in the Hills at Evening," in *The Oxford Book of Christian Verse*, ed. Lord David Cecil (Oxford: Clarendon Press, 1940), 520.

TRUE TO THE TRUST

10

MIRACLES OF THE RESTORATION

As I have begun my service in the holy apostleship, obviously my greatest thrill and the most joyful of all realizations is that I have the opportunity, as Nephi phrased it, to "talk of Christ, . . . rejoice in Christ, . . . preach of Christ, [and] prophesy of Christ" (2 Ne. 25:26) wherever I may be and with whomever I may find myself until the last breath of my life is gone. Surely there could be no higher purpose or greater privilege than that of "special [witness] of the name of Christ in all the world" (D&C 107:23).

But my greatest anxiety stems from that very same commission. A line of scripture reminds us with searing understatement that "they which preach the gospel should live . . . the gospel" (1 Cor. 9:14). Beyond my words and teachings and spoken witness, my life must be part of that testimony of Jesus. My very being should reflect the divinity of this work. I could not bear it if anything I might ever say or do would in any way diminish your faith in Christ, your love for this Church, or the esteem in which you hold the apostleship.

I know I cannot succeed without the guidance of the Master whose work this is. On occasion the beauty of His life and the magnitude of His gift comes to my heart with such force that, as a favorite hymn says, "I scarce can take it in."[1] The purity of His life, His mercy and compassion for us have led me again and again to "bow in humble adoration and there proclaim 'My God, how great thou art!'"

If I may, I wish to bear personal witness to a miracle I repeatedly see in the Church. That miracle is you, the great faithful but often unheralded body of the Church who play your part in the ongoing saga of the Restoration. In a real sense, the wonder and beauty of this historic day would not, could not, be complete without you.

Certainly I, for one, have taken great strength from you, you who come from a hundred different nations and ten hundred walks of life. You who have turned away from the glitter and glare and "vain imaginations" (1 Ne. 12:18) of the world, to seek a holier life in the splendor of the city of God. You who love your families and your neighbors and, yes, those who hate you and curse you and "despitefully use you, and persecute you" (Matt. 5:44). You who pay tithing with certainty even when you are uncertain about every other aspect of your financial future. You who send your sons and daughters on missions, clothing that child in better apparel than you now wear—or will wear—for the eighteen or twenty-four months of sacrifice that lie ahead. You who plead for blessings to be bestowed on others, especially those in physical or spiritual distress, offering to give them your own health or happiness if that would be something God could allow. You who face life alone, or face it without advantage, or face it with little success. You who carry on in quiet courage, doing the best you can. I pay tribute to every one of you and am deeply honored to stand in your presence.

I especially thank you for sustaining your leaders, whatever their personal sense of limitation may be. At each general conference, in common consent, you volunteer to uphold—or more literally "hold up"—the presiding officers of the kingdom, those who bear the keys and responsibility for the work, not one man of whom sought the position or feels equal to the task. And even when Jeffrey Holland's name is proposed as the last and the least of the newly ordained, your arm goes lovingly to the square. And you say to Brother Holland through his tears and his nights of walking the floor: "You lean on us. Lean on us out here in Omaha and Ontario and Osaka where we have never even seen you, and scarcely know who you are. But you are one of the 'Brethren,' so you are no stranger or foreigner to us, but a fellow citizen in the household of God. You will be prayed for in our family, and you will hold a place within our hearts. Our strength shall be your strength. Our faith will build your faith. Your work will be our work."

This Church, the great institutional body of Christ, is a marvelous work and a wonder not only because of what it does for the faithful but also because of what the faithful do for it. Your lives are at the very heart of that marvel. You are evidence of the wonder of it all.

Just twenty-four hours after my call as an Apostle, I left for a Church assignment in southern California where, in due course, I found myself standing by the bedsides of Debbie, Tanya, and Liza Avila. These three lovely sisters, aged thirty-three, thirty-two, and twenty-three, respectively, each developed muscular dystrophy at age seven. Since that tender age, each has had her rendezvous with pneumonia and tracheotomies, with neuropathy and leg braces. Then came wheelchairs, respirators, and, finally, total immobility.

Enduring the longest period of immobility of the three sisters, Tanya has been on her back for seventeen years, having never moved from her bed during that period of time. Never once in seventeen years has she seen the sun rise or set or felt the rain upon her face. Never once in seventeen years has she picked a flower or chased a rainbow or watched a bird in flight. For a lesser number of years, Debbie and Liza have also now lived with those same physical restrictions. Yet somehow through it all, these sisters have not only endured, they have triumphed—earning Young Women personal achievement awards, graduating from high school (including seminary), completing university correspondence courses, and reading the standard works over and over and over again.

But there has been one other abiding ambition these remarkable women were determined to see fulfilled. They rightly saw themselves as daughters of the covenant, offspring of Abraham and Sarah, Isaac and Rebekah, and Jacob and Rachel. They vowed that somehow, some way, someday they would go to the house of the Lord to claim those eternal promises. And now even that has been accomplished. "It was the most thrilling and fulfilling day of my life," Debbie said. "I truly felt I was home. Everyone was so gracious and helpful with the innumerable and seemingly insurmountable arrangements that had to be made. Never in my life have I felt more loved and accepted."

Of her experience, Tanya said: "The temple is the only place I have ever been where I felt truly whole. I have always felt I was a daughter of God, but only in the temple did I understand what that truly meant. The fact that I went through the experience lying horizontally with a respirator took absolutely nothing away from this sacred experience."

Elder Douglas Callister, who, along with the presidency and workers in the Los Angeles Temple, assisted these sisters in making their dream come true, said to me, "There they were, dressed in white, long black hair falling down nearly to the floor from their horizontal position, eyes filled with tears, unable to move their hands or any other part of the body except their heads, savoring, absorbing, cherishing every word, every moment, every aspect of the temple endowment." Debbie would later say of the experience, "I now know what it will be like to be resurrected, surrounded by heavenly angels, and in the presence of God."

One year after her own endowment, Debbie Avila made her way back to the temple, again with staggering special arrangements and assistance, to do the work for her beloved grandmother, who had literally given her life in the care of these three granddaughters. For twenty-two consecutive years, without reprieve or respite or exception, Sister Esperanza Lamelas cared for these three day and night. Virtually every night for twenty-two years, she awakened each hour on the hour to physically turn each child so that she would be comfortable in her sleep and avoid the problem of bedsores. In 1989, at age seventy-four, her own health now broken, she died, having given new meaning to the Prophet Joseph's invitation to "waste and wear out our lives . . . do[ing] all things that lie in our power . . . [for the benefit of] the rising generation, and . . . all the pure in heart" (D&C 123:13, 17, 11).

The ongoing miracle of the Restoration. Covenants.

Temples. Quiet, unsung Christian living. The work of the kingdom done with worn hands, weary hands, hands which in some cases cannot be raised to the square, but which are surely sustaining hands in every holy and sacred sense of the word.

Let me close.

The mid-1600s were a terrible time in England. The Puritan revolutionaries had executed a king, and political life—including Parliament—was in total chaos. A typhus epidemic turned the whole island into a hospital. The great plague, followed by the great fire, would turn it into a morgue.

In Leicestershire, near where Sister Holland and I lived and labored for three magnificent years, there is a very small church with a plaque on the wall which reads: "In the year of 1653, when all things sacred were . . . either demolished or profaned, Sir Robert Shirley, [built] this church; whose singular praise it is, To have done the best things in the worst times, and hoped them in the most calamitous."

To have done the best things in the worst times, and to have hoped them in the most calamitous. Those are lines I would use to praise the prophets *and* the faithful members of the Church of Jesus Christ down through the years—legions of the quietly heroic in every decade of the dispensation, led by the Lord's anointed, whose arms can also grow weary and whose legs are sometimes weak.

In the spirit of that legacy from those who have given so much—prophets and apostles and people like you—I pledge to "press forward with a steadfastness in Christ, having a perfect brightness of hope, and a love of God and of all men" (2 Ne. 31:20). I pledge to "take hold of that for which Christ once took hold of me."[2]

I testify of Him, the Redeemer of the world and Master of

106

us all. He is the Only Begotten Son of the living God, who has exalted that son's name over every other and has given Him principality, power, might, and dominion at His right hand in the heavenly place. We esteem this Messiah to be "holy, harmless, undefiled"—the bearer of "unchangeable priesthood" (Heb. 7:26, 24). He is the anchor to our souls and our high priest of promise. He is our God of good things to come. In time and in eternity—and surely in striving to fulfill this responsibility which has come to me—I shall forever be grateful for His promise: "I will never leave thee, nor forsake thee" (Heb. 13:5). I thank Him for that blessing upon us all.

Notes

From a talk given at general conference, October 1994.

1. Stuart K. Hine, "How Great Thou Art," in *Hymns of The Church of Jesus Christ of Latter-day Saints* (Salt Lake City: The Church of Jesus Christ of Latter-day Saints, 1985), no. 86.
2. New English Bible, Philippians 3:12.

11

CALLED TO SERVE

As did many of you, I grew up on the stories of the early Brethren going on missions to Canada, England, Scandinavia, continental Europe, the Pacific Islands, Mexico, Asia, and so on. More recently I have read of Parley P. Pratt's brief mission to Chile, where the Pratts lost and buried their infant son at Valparaíso. I have read of Elder Melvin J. Ballard, who was called to dedicate South America when that marvelous continent was still one new and rather overwhelming mission field. The service which builds a young, growing Church is not casually requested nor whimsically given. On occasion the obstacles have been great and the price sometimes very dear.

And we speak not only of those early Brethren who went out to serve, but the women who supported them—and in addition supported themselves and their children, staying at home to raise and protect families, that other portion of the Lord's vineyard about which He is so emphatic.

On the day of her husband's second departure to England, Vilate Kimball was so weak, trembling so severely with ague, that she could do nothing more than weakly shake hands with her husband when he came in tears to say good-bye. Their little David was less than four weeks old then, and only one child, four-year-old Heber Parley, was well enough to carry water for the ailing family. In the hours after her husband's leaving, Vilate lost all strength and had to be assisted back to the confinement of her bed.

Mary Ann Young and her children were equally ill when Brigham left on the same mission, and their financial situation was equally precarious. One heartrending account describes her crossing the Mississippi River in the bitter of winter, thinly clad and shivering with cold, clutching her infant daughter as she went, going to the tithing office in Nauvoo to ask for a few potatoes. Then, still suffering with fever, she made her way with the baby back across the forbidding river, never to write a word to her husband about such difficulties.[1]

We seldom face anything like those circumstances today, though many missionaries and members still sacrifice greatly to do the work of the Lord. As blessings come and the Church matures, we all hope that service will never be so difficult as these early members found it, but as missionaries are singing this day from Oslo to Osorno and from Seattle to Cebu, we *are* "called to serve."[2] To raise our families and serve faithfully in the Church, all without running faster than we have strength (see Mosiah 4:27), require wisdom, judgment, divine help—and inevitably some sacrifice. From Adam to the present hour, true faith in the Lord Jesus Christ has always been linked to the offering of sacrifice, our small gift to be a symbolic echo of His majestic offering.[3] With his eye firmly on the Atonement of Jesus Christ, the Prophet Joseph Smith taught that a religion that does not include covenants of sacrifice cannot have the power to bring the promise of eternal life.[4]

May I share just one contemporary example of both the challenge and blessings that our "calls to serve" can bring. A wonderful sister recently said to a dear friend: "I want to tell you about the moment I ceased resenting my husband's time and sacrifice as a bishop. It had seemed uncanny how an 'emergency' would arise with a ward member just when he and I were about to go out to do something special together.

"One day I poured out my frustration, and my husband agreed we should guarantee, in addition to Monday nights, one additional night a week just for us. Well, the first 'date night' came, and we were about to get into the car for an evening together when the telephone rang.

" 'This is a test,' I smiled at him. The telephone kept ringing. 'Remember our agreement. Remember our date. Remember me. Let the phone ring.' In the end I wasn't smiling.

"My poor husband looked trapped between me and a ringing telephone. I really did know that his highest loyalty was to me, and I knew he wanted that evening as much as I did. But he seemed paralyzed by the sound of that telephone.

" 'I'd better at least check,' he said with sad eyes. 'It is probably nothing at all.'

" 'If you do, our date is ruined,' I cried. 'I just know it.'

"He squeezed my hand and said, 'Be right back,' and he dashed in to pick up the telephone.

"Well, when my husband didn't return to the car immediately, I knew what was happening. I got out of the car, went into the house, and went to bed. The next morning he spoke a quiet apology, I spoke an even quieter acceptance, and that was the end of it.

"Or so I thought. I found the event still bothering me several weeks later. I wasn't blaming my husband, but I was disappointed nevertheless. The memory was still fresh when I came upon a woman in the ward I scarcely knew. Very hesitantly, she asked for the opportunity to talk. She then told of becoming infatuated with another man, who seemed to bring excitement into her life of drudgery, she with a husband who worked full-time and carried a full load of classes at the university. Their apartment was confining. She had small children who were often demanding, noisy, and exhausting. She said: 'I was sorely tempted to leave what I saw as my wretched state and just go with this man. My situation was such that I felt I deserved better than what I had. My rationalization persuaded me to think I could walk away from my husband, my children, my temple covenants, and my Church and find happiness with a stranger.'

"She said: 'The plan was set; the time for my escape was agreed upon. Yet, as if in a last gasp of sanity, my conscience told me to call your husband, my bishop. I say "conscience," but I know that was a spiritual prompting directly from heaven. Almost against my will, I called. The telephone rang and rang and rang. Such was the state of my mind that I actually thought, "If the bishop doesn't answer, that will be a sign I should go through with my plan." The phone kept ringing, and I was about to hang up and walk straight into destruction when suddenly I heard your husband's voice. It penetrated my soul like lightning. Suddenly I heard myself sobbing, saying, "Bishop, is that you? I am in trouble. I need help." Your husband came with help, and I am safe today because he answered that telephone.

" 'I look back and realize I was tired and foolish and vulnerable. I love my husband and my children with all my heart. I can't imagine the tragedy my life would be without them. These are still demanding times for our family. I know everyone has them. But we have addressed some of these issues, and things are looking brighter. They always do eventually.' Then she said: 'I don't know you well, but I wish to thank you for supporting your husband in his calling. I don't know what the cost for such service has been to you or to your children, but if on a difficult day there is a particularly personal cost, please know how eternally grateful I will be for the sacrifice people like you make to help rescue people like me.' "

Please understand that I am one who preaches emphatically a more manageable, more realistic expectation of what our bishops and other leaders can do. I especially feel that a wide range of civic, professional, and other demands which take parents, including and especially mothers, out of homes where children are being raised is among the most serious problems in contemporary society. And because I am adamant about spouses and children deserving sacred, committed time with a husband and father, nine times out of ten I would have been right alongside that wife telling her husband *not* to answer that telephone. But I am as grateful in my own way as that young woman was in hers that in this instance this good man followed the prompting of the Spirit and responded to his "call"—in this case, literally—his "call to serve."

I testify of home and family and marriage, the most precious human possessions of our lives. I testify of the need to protect and preserve them while we find time and ways to serve faithfully in the Church. In what I hope are rare moments when these seem to be in conflict, when we find an hour or a day or a night of crisis when duty and spiritual prompting require our response, in those situations I pay tribute to every wife who has ever sat alone while dinner got cold, every husband who has made his own dinner, which with him as cook was bound to be cold anyway, and every child who has ever been disappointed in a postponed camping trip or a ball game a parent unexpectedly had to miss (and that better not be very often!). I pay tribute to every mission president and his wife, their children, and every senior couple called to serve with them, and all others who for a season miss births and baptisms, weddings and funerals, family and fun experiences in response to a "call to serve." I thank all who, in challenging circumstances across the Church, do the best they can to build the kingdom of God on earth.

I testify of the sacrifice and service of the Lord Jesus Christ, who gave everything for us and in that spirit of giving said "follow thou me" (John 21:22). "If any man serve me, let him follow me," He said, "and where I am, there shall also my servant be: if any man serve me, him will my Father honour" (John 12:26). Such service inevitably brings challenging decisions about how to balance priorities and how best to be the disciples He wishes us to be. I thank Him for His divine guidance in helping us make those decisions and for assisting us to find the right way for all concerned. I thank Him that "he has borne our griefs, and carried our sorrows" (Mosiah 14:4; see Isa. 53:4) and that He has called us to do some of the same for each other.

Notes

From a talk given at general conference, October 2002.

1. For the definitive work documenting these experiences, see James B. Allen, Ronald K. Esplin, and David J. Whittaker, *Men with a Mission: The Quorum of the Twelve Apostles in the British Isles, 1837–1841* (Salt

Lake City: Deseret Book, 1992). The suffering of Vilate Kimball and Mary Ann Young is noted on pages 267–76.

2. Grace Gordon, "Called to Serve," in *Hymns of The Church of Jesus Christ of Latter-day Saints* (Salt Lake City: The Church of Jesus Christ of Latter-day Saints, 1985), no. 249.

3. This is a major doctrine too expansive for documentation here. See Moses 5:4–8; 3 Nephi 9:17–21; D&C 59:8–12; 97:8–9.

4. See Joseph Smith, *Lectures on Faith* (Salt Lake City: Deseret Book, 1985), 68–69.

12

"SANCTIFY YOURSELVES"

This message is intended for all of us, whatever our age or years of service, but I do wish to speak specifically to the deacons, teachers, and priests in the Aaronic Priesthood and to the young, newly ordained elders in the Melchizedek Priesthood—you of the rising generation, you who must be ready to use your priesthood, often at times and in ways you did not anticipate.

In that spirit, my call to you is something of the call Joshua gave to an earlier generation of priesthood bearers, young men and those not so young, who needed to perform a miracle in their time. To these who would need to complete ancient Israel's most formidable task—recapturing and repossessing their promised land of old—Joshua said, "Sanctify yourselves: for to morrow the Lord will do wonders among you" (Josh. 3:5).

Let me share a story with you suggesting how soon and how unexpectedly those tomorrows can come and in some cases

how little time you may have to make hasty, belated preparation.

On the afternoon of Wednesday, September 30, 1998, a
Little League football team in Inkom, Idaho, was out on the
field for its midweek practice. They had completed their warm-
ups and were starting to run a few plays from scrimmage. Dark
clouds were gathering, as they sometimes do in the fall, and it
began to rain lightly, but that was of no concern to a group of
boys who loved playing football.

Suddenly, seemingly out of nowhere, an absolutely deafen-
ing crack of thunder split the air, inseparable from the flash of
lightning that illuminated, literally electrified, the entire scene.

At that very moment a young friend of mine, A. J. Edwards,
then a deacon in the Portneuf Ward of the McCammon Idaho
Stake, was ready for the ball on a handoff that was sure to be a
touchdown in this little intersquad bit of horseplay. But the
lightning that had illuminated earth and sky struck A. J.
Edwards from the crown of his football helmet to the soles of
his shoes.

The impact of the strike stunned all the players, knocking a
few to the ground, leaving one player temporarily without his
sight and virtually all the rest of the players dazed and shaken.
Instinctively they started running for the concrete pavilion
adjacent to the park. Some of the boys began to cry. Many of
them fell to their knees and began to pray. Through it all, A. J.
Edwards lay motionless on the field.

Brother David Johnson of the Rapid Creek Ward, McCammon
Idaho Stake, rushed to the player's side. He shouted to coach
and fellow ward member Rex Shaffer, "I can't get a pulse. He's
in cardiac arrest." These two men, rather miraculously both

trained emergency medical technicians, started a life-against-death effort in CPR.

Cradling A. J.'s head as the men worked was the young defensive coach of the team, eighteen-year-old Bryce Reynolds, a member of the Mountain View Ward, McCammon Idaho Stake. As he watched Brother Johnson and Brother Shaffer urgently applying CPR, he had an impression. I am confident it was a revelation from heaven in every sense of the word. He remembered vividly a priesthood blessing that the bishop had once given his grandfather following an equally tragic and equally life-threatening accident years earlier. Now, as he held this young deacon in his arms, he realized that for the first time in his life he needed to use his newly conferred Melchizedek Priesthood in a similar way. In anticipation of his nineteenth birthday and forthcoming call to serve a mission, young Bryce Reynolds had been ordained an elder just thirty-nine days earlier.

Whether he audibly spoke the words or only uttered them under his breath, Elder Reynolds said: "A. J. Edwards, in the name of the Lord Jesus Christ and by the power and authority of the Melchizedek Priesthood which I hold, I bless you that you will be OK. In the name of Jesus Christ, amen." As Bryce Reynolds closed that brief but fervent blessing offered in the language of an eighteen-year-old, A. J. Edwards drew his first renewed breath.

The ongoing prayers, miracles, and additional priesthood blessings of that entire experience—including a high-speed ambulance drive to Pocatello and a near-hopeless LifeFlight to the burn center at the University of Utah—all of that the Edwards family can share with us at a later time. It is sufficient to say that a very healthy and very robust A. J. Edwards is in the audience tonight with his father as my special guests. I also recently talked on the telephone with Elder Bryce Reynolds, who has been serving faithfully in the Texas Dallas Mission for the past seventeen months. I love these two wonderful young men.

Now, my young friends of both the Aaronic and Melchizedek Priesthood, not every prayer is answered so immediately, and not every priesthood declaration can command the renewal or the sustaining of life. Sometimes the will of God is otherwise. But young men, you will learn, if you have not already, that in frightening, even perilous moments, your faith and your priesthood will demand the very best of you and the best you can call down from heaven. You Aaronic Priesthood boys will not use your priesthood in exactly the same way an ordained elder uses the Melchizedek Priesthood, but all priesthood bearers must be instruments in the hand of God, and to be so, you must, as Joshua said, "Sanctify yourselves." You must be ready and worthy to act.

That is why the Lord repeatedly says in the scriptures, "Be ye clean, that bear the vessels of the Lord" (Isa. 52:11; see 3 Ne. 20:41; D&C 38:42; 133:5). Let me tell you what that phrase "bear the vessels of the Lord" means. Anciently it had at least two meanings, both related to the work of the priesthood.

The first refers to the recovery and return to Jerusalem of various temple implements that had been carried into Babylon by King Nebuchadnezzar. In physically handling the return of these items, the Lord reminded those early brethren of the sanctity of anything related to the temple. Therefore as they carried back to their homeland these various bowls, basins, cups, and other vessels, they themselves were to be as clean as the ceremonial instruments they bore (see 2 Kgs. 25:14–15; Ezra 1:5–11).

The second meaning is related to the first. Similar bowls and implements were used for ritual purification in the home. The Apostle Paul, writing to his young friend Timothy, said of these, "In a great house there are . . . vessels of gold and of silver, . . . of wood and of earth"—these means of washing and cleansing common in the time of the Savior. But Paul goes on to say, "If a man . . . purge himself [of unworthiness], *he* shall *be* a vessel . . . sanctified, and meet for the master's use, and prepared unto every good work." Therefore, Paul says, "Flee . . . youthful lusts: . . . follow righteousness, . . . call on the Lord out of a pure heart" (2 Tim. 2:20–22; emphasis added).

In both of these biblical accounts, the message is that as priesthood bearers not only are we to *handle* sacred vessels and emblems of God's power—think of preparing, blessing, and passing the sacrament, for example—but we are also to *be* a sanctified instrument as well. Partly because of what we are to *do* but more importantly because of what we are to *be*, the prophets and apostles tell us to "flee . . . youthful lusts" and "call on the Lord out of a pure heart." They tell us to be clean.

Now, we live in an age when that cleanliness is more and more difficult to preserve. With modern technology even your youngest brothers and sisters can be carried virtually around the world before they are old enough to ride a tricycle safely across the street. What were in my generation carefree moments of moviegoing, TV watching, and magazine reading have now, with the additional availability of VCRs, the Internet, and personal computers, become *amusements* fraught with genuine moral danger. I put the word *amusements* in italics. Did you know that the original Latin meaning of the word *amusement* is "a diversion of the mind intended to deceive"? Unfortunately that is largely what "amusements" in our day have again become in the hands of the arch deceiver.

Recently I read an author who said: "Our leisure, even our play, is a matter of serious concern. [That is because] there is no neutral ground in the universe: every square inch, every split second, is claimed by God and counterclaimed by Satan."[1] I believe that to be absolutely true, and no such claiming and counterclaiming anywhere is more crucial and conspicuous than that being waged for the minds and morals, the personal purity of the young.

Brethren, part of my warning voice tonight is that this will only get worse. It seems the door to permissiveness, the door to lewdness and vulgarity and obscenity swings only one way. It only opens farther and farther; it never seems to swing back. Individuals can choose to close it, but it is certain, historically speaking, that public appetite and public policy will not close it. No, in the moral realm the only real control you have is self-control.

Brethren, if you are struggling with self-control in what you look at or listen to, in what you say or what you do, I ask you to pray to your Father in Heaven for help. Pray to Him as Enos did, who wrestled before God and struggled mightily in the spirit (see Enos 1:2–10). Wrestle like Jacob did with the angel, refusing to let go until a blessing had come (see Gen. 32:24–26). Talk to your mom and dad. Talk to your bishop. Get the best help you can from all the good people who surround you. Avoid at all costs others who would tempt you, weaken your will, or perpetuate the problem. If anyone does not feel fully worthy tonight, he can become worthy through repentance and the Atonement of the Lord Jesus Christ. The Savior wept and bled and died for you. He has given everything for your happiness and salvation. He certainly is not going to withhold help from you now!

Then you can help others to whom you are sent, now and in the future, as one holding the priesthood of God. You can then, as a missionary, be what the Lord described as "a physician unto the church" (D&C 31:10).

Young men, we love you. We worry about you and want to help you every way we can. Nearly two hundred years ago, William Wordsworth wrote that "the world is too much with us." What on earth would he say about the encroachments pressing in on your souls and sensibilities today? In addressing some of these problems facing you, we are mindful that an absolute multitude of young men is faithfully living the gospel and standing resolutely before the Lord. I am sure that multitude includes the overwhelming majority of all who are listening here tonight. But the cautions we give to the few are important reminders even to the faithful.

In the most difficult and discouraging days of World War II, Winston Churchill said to the people of England: "To every man there comes . . . that special moment when he is figuratively tapped on the shoulder and offered the chance to do a special thing unique to him and fitted to his talent. What a tragedy if that moment finds him unprepared or unqualified for the work which would be his finest hour."

In an even more serious kind of spiritual warfare, brethren, the day may come—indeed, I am certain *will* come—when in an unexpected circumstance or a time of critical need, lightning will strike, so to speak, and the future will be in your hands. Be ready when that day comes. Be strong. Always be clean. Respect and revere the priesthood that you hold, tonight and forever. I

123

bear witness of this work, of the power we have been given to direct it, and of the need to be worthy in administering it. Brethren, I testify that the call in every age—and especially our age—is Joshua's call: "Sanctify yourselves: for to morrow the Lord will do wonders among you."

Notes

From a talk given at general conference, October 2000.

1.   C. S. Lewis, *Christian Reflections*, ed. Walter Hooper (Grand Rapids, Mich.: W. B. Eerdmans, 1967), 33.

13

OUR PRIESTHOOD LEGACY

In this message I wish to speak rather directly to the young men of the Church, bearers of the Aaronic Priesthood. I wish to impress upon you some sense of history, something of what it has meant, something of what it may yet mean, to belong to the true and living church of God and hold the significant offices in its priesthood that you now hold and will yet hold.

So much that we do in this Church is directed toward you, those whom the Book of Mormon calls "the rising generation" (Mosiah 26:1; Alma 5:49). We who have already walked that portion of life's path that you are now on try to call back to you something of what we have learned. We shout encouragement. We try to warn of pitfalls or perils along the way. Where possible we try to walk with you and keep you close to our side.

Believe it or not we, too, were young once, though I know that strains the very limits of your imagination. Equally unfathomable is the fact that your parents were once young also, and so were your bishops and your quorum advisers. But as the years have gone by we have learned many lessons beyond those of youth—that, for example, Noah's wife was *not* named Joan of Arc, and, so far as we know, Pontius Pilate flew no commercial aircraft of any kind. Why do you think we now try so hard and worry so much and want the very best for you? It is because we have been your age and you have never been ours, and we have learned some things you do not yet know.

When you are young not all of life's questions and difficulties have arisen yet, but they will arise, and unfortunately, for your generation, they will arise at a younger and younger age. The gospel of Jesus Christ marks the only sure and safe path. So older men, seasoned men—men passing on to you the legacy of history—continue to call out to youth.

This call from one generation to another is one of the reasons we hold priesthood meetings with dads seated next to sons, and priesthood leaders at the side of those whose fathers may be absent. It was in a stake priesthood meeting with a format very much like this one that the then twelve-year-old Gordon B. Hinckley stood in the back of the old Salt Lake Tenth Ward building—his first such stake priesthood meeting as a newly ordained deacon—feeling just a bit lonely and a little out of place.

But upon hearing the men of that stake sing W. W. Phelps's stirring memorial tribute "Praise to the Man," this young boy, who would one day be a prophet himself, had it borne upon his soul that Joseph Smith *was indeed* a prophet of God, that he had in truth "communed with Jehovah," that "millions shall know 'Brother Joseph' again."[1] Yes, some part of the preparation for this future prophet began when a twelve-year-old deacon heard

126

faithful, experienced, older men sing the hymns of Zion in a priesthood meeting.

Now very few twelve-year-olds will live to become the president of the Church, nor do we need to in order to prove our faithfulness. But let us never forget that "in every place a man now stands, a boy once used to be," and all of you young men have the opportunity—and the responsibility—to be just as faithful in gaining a testimony and standing for the truth as did the men we have sustained as prophets, seers, and revelators down through the dispensations. Indeed, this is one of those things history calls out to us—that the future may be daunting, but you young men are more than equal to the task.

The name Rudger Clawson will, unfortunately, be unfamiliar to many of you. For forty-five years Brother Clawson was a member of the Quorum of the Twelve Apostles, and for twenty-two of those years served as the president of that quorum. But long before any of those responsibilities came to him, he had a chance to prove his faithfulness and demonstrate in his youth just how willing he was to defend his beliefs, even at the peril of his life.

As a young man Brother Clawson had been called on a mission to the Southern States. At that time in America's history, well over one hundred years ago, malicious mobs were still in existence, outlaws who threatened the safety of members of the Church and others. Elder Clawson and his missionary companion, Elder Joseph Standing, were traveling on foot to a missionary conference when, nearing their destination, they were suddenly confronted by twelve armed and angry men on horseback.

With cocked rifles and revolvers shoved in their faces, the two elders were repeatedly struck and occasionally knocked to the ground as they were led away from their prescribed path and forced to walk deep into the nearby woods. Elder Joseph Standing, knowing what might lie in store for them, made a bold move and seized a pistol within his reach. Instantly one of the assailants turned his gun on young Standing and fired. Another mobber, pointing to Elder Clawson, said, "Shoot that man." In response every weapon in the circle was turned on him.

It seemed to this young elder that his fate was to be the same as that of his fallen brother. He said: "I . . . at once realized there was no avenue of escape. My time had come. . . . My turn to follow Joseph Standing was at hand." He folded his arms, looked his assailants in the face, and said, "Shoot."

Whether stunned by this young elder's courage or now fearfully aware of what they had already done to his companion, we cannot know, but someone in that fateful moment shouted, "Don't shoot," and one by one the guns were lowered. Terribly shaken but driven by loyalty to his missionary companion, Elder Clawson continued to defy the mob. Never certain that he might not yet be shot, young Rudger, often working and walking with his back to the mob, was able to carry the body of his slain companion to a safe haven where he performed the last act of kindness for his fallen friend. There he gently washed the bloody stains from the missionary's body and prepared it for the long train ride home.[2]

I tell that story with some concern, hoping no one will dwell on the death of a young missionary or think gospel living brought only trials or tragedies in those early years. But I do share it for an ever younger and ever newer generation in the Church who may not know the gifts earlier men and women— including young men and women—have given us in what one

Church-produced film states simply in another single word—
Legacy.

Fortunately we do not, for the most part, face any such
physical threats now. No, for the most part, our courage will be
more quiet, less dramatic, but in every way as crucial and as
demanding. May I use one example drawn from contemporary
history, an example demonstrating faith and loyalty more like
that which you and I will be called upon to exhibit. In doing so,
I pay tribute to faithful fathers who serve as the standard of
strength for their growing and less-experienced sons.

Some years ago, long after he had returned from his mission,
Bishop J. Richard Yates, of the Durham Third Ward in the
Durham North Carolina Stake, was out on the family farm in
Idaho, helping his father milk the cows and do some of the
evening chores. Because of limited family circumstances,
Richard's father, Brother Tom Yates, had not been able to go on
a mission in his youth. But that disappointment only strength-
ened Brother Yates's vow that what he had not been able to
afford, his sons would certainly realize—a full-time mission for
the Lord—whatever the sacrifice involved.

In those days in rural Idaho, it was customary to give a
young man a heifer calf as soon as he was old enough to take
care of it. The idea was that the young man would raise the ani-
mal, keep some of the offspring, and sell others to help pay for
the feed. Fathers wisely understood that this was a way to teach
their sons responsibility as they earned money for their missions.

Young Richard did well with that gift of a first calf and, over
time, expanded the herd to eight. Along the way he invested
some of the income from the milk he sold to buy a litter of pigs.
He had nearly sixty of those when his call finally arrived. It was
the family's plan that they would sell future litters of the pigs to

supplement income from the sale of the dairy milk to cover the costs of Richard's missionary labors.

That evening out in the barn long after a wonderful twenty-four months was safely concluded, this young man heard something of which he had known absolutely nothing while on his mission. His father said that sometime within the first month after Richard had left, the local veterinarian, a close family friend and tireless worker in that farming community, had come to vaccinate the pigs against a local threat of cholera. But in an unfortunate professional error, the vet gave the animals the live vaccine but failed to give adequate antiserum. The results were that the entire herd of pigs came down with the disease; within a few weeks most of the animals were dead, and the remaining few had to be destroyed.

With the pigs dead, obviously milk sales would not be enough to keep Richard on his mission, so his father planned to sell one by one the family's dairy herd to cover the costs. But beginning with the second month and virtually every month for twenty-three thereafter, as his parents prepared to send him the money for his mission, either one of their cows suddenly died or else one of his did. Thus the herd decreased at twice the rate they expected. It seemed an unbelievable stretch of misfortune.

During that difficult time, a large note became due at the local bank. With all else that had happened and the inordinate financial problems they were facing, Brother Yates simply did not have the money to repay it. There was every likelihood they would now lose their entire farm. After much prayer and concern, but with never a word to their missionary son, Brother Yates went to face the president of the bank, a man not of our faith who was perceived in the community to be somewhat stern and quite aloof.

After he had heard the explanation of this considerable misfortune, the banker sat for a moment, looking into the face of a man who, in his own quiet and humble way, was standing up to trouble and opposition and fear as faithfully as had Rudger Clawson and Joseph Standing. In that situation I suppose Brother Yates could not say much more to his banker than "Shoot."

Quietly the bank president leaned forward and asked just one question. "Tom," he said, "are you paying your tithing?" Not at all certain as to how the answer would be received, Brother Yates answered softly but without hesitation, "Yes, sir, I am." The banker then said, "You keep paying your tithing, and you keep your son on his mission. I'll take care of the note. I know you will repay me when you can."

No paperwork or signatures were exchanged. No threats or warnings were uttered. Two good and honorable men simply stood and shook hands. An agreement had been made and that agreement was kept.

Bishop Yates says he remembers hearing this heretofore unknown story with considerable emotion that evening, asking his father—the note to the bank long since repaid—if all that worry and fear and sacrifice had been worth it just to try to live the gospel and keep a son on a mission. "Yes, Son," he said, "it was worth all of that and a lot more if the Lord ever asks it of me," and he continued with his evening chores.

Physically, Tom Yates was a slight man—under five feet eight inches in height and weighing less than 150 pounds. His body was stunted somewhat from a near-fatal case of polio contracted in his infancy. But Richard says he does not ever remember thinking of his father's physical stature, one way or the other. To this son he was simply a spiritual giant, always larger than life, leaving his children a legacy of devotion and courage longer than all eternity.

To such fathers of our families and fathers of our faith, to those who have lived lives of integrity whatever the cost, to generations in this and every dispensation who've faced fear and trials and, yes, death unflinchingly, I express gratitude from the bottom of my heart. I commend you young men for what must be your determination to live the gospel of Jesus Christ. I shoulder with you the responsibility placed on each one of us who bears the priesthood of God. I plead for each of us to remember that in the work of the Lord we must often turn our cheek, but we must never turn our coat. I pledge with you my own determination to be true and faithful to the Lord Jesus Christ whose church this is, even as I praise with you that legacy of loyalty given to us by those who have gone before, in the sacred name of Jesus Christ, amen.

Notes

From a talk given at general conference, April 1995.

1. William W. Phelps, "Praise to the Man," in *Hymns of The Church of Jesus Christ of Latter-day Saints* (Salt Lake City: The Church of Jesus Christ of Latter-day Saints, 1985), no. 27.
2. In David S. Hoopes and Roy Hoopes, *The Making of a Mormon Apostle: The Story of Rudger Clawson* (New York: Madison Books, 1990), 23–31.

14

"As Doves to Our Windows"

These are surely some of the days which our faithful and
farsighted ancestors saw in the earliest years of the
Restoration. In a general conference of the Church in
April 1844, the brethren recalled those first gatherings of 1830.
One of them said: "We [talked] about the kingdom of God as if
we had the world at our command; we talked with great confidence, and talked big things, although we were not many [in
number]; . . . we looked [and] if we did not see *this* [congrega-
tion], we saw by vision, the church of God, a thousand times
larger [than it was then], although [at the time] we were not
enough to well man a farm, or meet a woman with a milk pail.
. . . All the members [of the Church] met in conference, in a
room 20 feet square. . . . We talked about . . . people coming as
doves to the windows, that all nations should flock unto [the
Church]. . . . If we had told the people what our eyes behold this
day, we should not [have been] believed."[1]

If this was their feeling in that fateful year of 1844, just prior to Joseph Smith's martyrdom, what must those same brethren and sisters see from their eternal home on a day like this, when we are 11 million strong and meet in this marvelous Conference Center! So much has happened since then for which they and we need to be grateful. And, of course, this is not the end. We have much work yet to do, in both the quality and quantity of our faithfulness and our service. George A. Smith, counselor in the First Presidency to President Brigham Young, once said by way of caution, "We may build temples, erect stately domes, magnificent spires [and] grand towers, in honor of our religion, but if we fail to live the principles of that religion . . . , and to acknowledge God in all our thoughts, we shall fall short of the blessings which its practical exercise would ensure."[2] We must be humble and conscientious. The honor and the glory of all that is good goes to God, and there is much still ahead of us that will be refining, even difficult, as He leads us from strength to strength.

In all of this my mind has turned to those early Saints who are too often lost to history, those who quietly and faithfully bore the kingdom forward through far more difficult days. So many of them seem almost nameless to us now. Most went unheralded to their graves—often early graves. Some few have made it into a line or two of Church history, but most have come and gone with neither high office nor history's regard. These folks, our collective ancestors, slipped into eternity as quietly and anonymously as they lived their religion. These are the silent Saints of whom President J. Reuben Clark once spoke when he thanked them all, "especially," he said, "the meekest and lowliest of them, [largely] unknown [and] unremembered, [except] round the hearthstones of their children and their

children's children who pass down from generation to generation the story of their faith."[3]

Whether longtime member or newest of converts, we are all
the beneficiaries of such faithful forebears. Perhaps it has always
been so down through the dispensations. Jesus once reminded
His disciples that they were reaping in fields wherein they had
bestowed no labor (see John 4:38). Moses had said to his people
earlier:

"The Lord thy God shall [bring] thee into the land which
he sware unto thy fathers, . . . to give thee great and goodly
cities, which thou buildedst not,

"And houses full of all good things, which thou filledst not,
and wells digged, which thou diggedst not, vineyards and olive
trees, which thou plantedst not" (Deut. 6:10–11).

My mind goes back 167 years to a little handful of women,
older men, and those children that could labor who were left to
keep construction going on the Kirtland Temple while virtually
every man well enough to do so had undertaken a relief march
of 1,000 miles to aid the Saints in Missouri. The records indi-
cate that quite literally every woman in Kirtland was engaged
in knitting and spinning in order to clothe the men and boys
laboring on the temple.

Elder Heber C. Kimball wrote, "The Lord only knows the
scenes of poverty, tribulation, and distress which we passed
through in order to accomplish this." It was recorded that one
leader of the day, looking upon the suffering and poverty of the
Church, frequently went upon the walls of that building by day
and by night, weeping and crying aloud to the Almighty to send
means whereby they might finish that building.[4]

It was not any easier when the Saints moved west and began
to settle in these valleys. As a young man of Primary and

135

Aaronic Priesthood age, I attended church in the grand old St. George Tabernacle, construction for which had begun in 1863. During very lengthy sermons I would amuse myself by gazing about the building, admiring the marvelous pioneer craftsmanship that had built that striking facility. Did you know, by the way, that there are 184 clusters of grapes carved into the ceiling cornice of that building? (Some of those sermons were really long!) But most of all I enjoyed counting the window panes—2,244 of them—because I grew up on the story of Peter Neilson, one of those little-noted and now-forgotten Saints of whom we have been speaking.

In the course of constructing that tabernacle, the local brethren ordered the glass for the windows from New York and had it shipped around the cape to California. But a bill of $800 was due and payable before the panes could be picked up and delivered to St. George. Brother David H. Cannon, later to preside over the St. George Temple being built at the same time, was charged with the responsibility of raising the needed funds. After painstaking effort, the entire community, giving virtually everything they had to these two monumental building projects, had been able to come up with only $200 cash. On sheer faith Brother Cannon committed a team of freighters to prepare to leave for California to get the glass. He continued to pray that the enormous balance of $600 would somehow be forthcoming before their departure.

Living in nearby Washington, Utah, was Peter Neilson, a Danish immigrant who had been saving for years to add on to his modest two-room adobe home. On the eve of the freighters' departure for California, Peter spent a sleepless night in that tiny little house. He thought of his conversion in far-off Denmark and his subsequent gathering with the Saints in

America. After coming west he had settled and struggled to make a living in Sanpete. And then, just as some prosperity seemed imminent there, he answered the call to uproot and go to the Cotton Mission, bolstering the pathetic and sagging efforts of the alkali-soiled, malaria-plagued, flood-bedeviled settlers of Dixie. As he lay in bed that night contemplating his years in the Church, he weighed the sacrifices asked of him against the wonderful blessings he had received. Somewhere in those private hours, he made a decision.

Some say it was a dream, others say an impression, still others simply a call to duty. However the direction came, Peter Neilson arose before dawn on the morning the teams were to leave for California. With only a candle and the light of the gospel to aid him, Peter brought out of a secret hiding place $600 in gold coins—half eagles, eagles, and double eagles. His wife, Karen, aroused by the predawn bustling, asked why he was up so early. He said only that he had to walk quickly the seven miles to St. George.

As the first light of morning fell on the beautiful red cliffs of southern Utah, a knock came at David H. Cannon's door. There stood Peter Neilson, holding a red bandanna which sagged under the weight it carried. "Good morning, David," said Peter. "I hope I am not too late. You will know what to do with this money."

With that he turned on his heel and retraced his steps back to Washington, back to a faithful and unquestioning wife, and back to a small two-room adobe house that remained just two rooms for many years to come.[5]

One other account from those early, faithful builders of modern Zion. John R. Moyle lived in Alpine, Utah, about twenty-two miles as the crow flies to the Salt Lake Temple, where he was the chief superintendent of masonry during its construction. To make certain he was always at work by 8 o'clock, Brother Moyle would start walking about 2 A.M. on Monday mornings. He would finish his work week at 5 P.M. on Friday and then start the walk home, arriving there shortly before midnight. Each week he would repeat that schedule for the entire time he served on the construction of the temple.

Once when he was home on the weekend, one of his cows bolted during milking and kicked Brother Moyle in the leg, shattering the bone just below the knee. With no better medical help than they had in such rural circumstances, his family and friends took a door off the hinges and strapped him onto that makeshift operating table. They then took the bucksaw they had been using to cut branches from a nearby tree and amputated his leg just a few inches below the knee. When against all medical likelihood the leg finally started to heal, Brother Moyle took a piece of wood and carved an artificial leg. First he walked in the house. Then he walked around the yard. Finally he ventured out about his property. When he felt he could stand the pain, he strapped on his leg, walked the twenty-two miles to the Salt Lake Temple, climbed the scaffolding, and with a chisel in his hand hammered out the declaration "Holiness to the Lord."[6]

With the faith of our fathers and mothers so evident on every side today, may I close with the remainder of the passage I cited at the outset of my remarks. It seems particularly relevant in our wonderful circumstances today. After Moses had told that earlier generation of the blessings they enjoyed because of the faithfulness of those who had gone before them, he said:

"Then beware lest thou forget the Lord, which brought thee forth. . . .

"Ye shall not go after other gods, . . . the gods of the people which are round about you. . . .

"For thou art an holy people unto the Lord thy God: [he] hath chosen thee to be a special people unto himself. . . .

"[He] did not . . . choose you, because ye were more in number than any [other] people; for ye were the fewest of all people:

"But because [he] loved you, and because he would keep the oath which he had sworn unto your fathers. . . .

"Know therefore that the Lord . . . is God, the faithful God, which keepeth covenant and mercy with them that love him and keep his commandments to a thousand generations" (Deut. 6:12, 14; 7:6–9).

We are still being blessed by that love from God and by the faithfulness of our spiritual and literal progenitors down through a thousand generations. May we do as much with the blessings we have been given as they did out of the deprivations so many of them faced. In such abundance may we never "forget the Lord" nor "go after other gods," but always be "an holy people unto the Lord." If we do so, those that hunger and thirst for the word of the Lord will continue to come "as doves to [our] windows." They will come seeking peace and growth and salvation. If we live our religion, they will find all of that and more.

We are a blessed people. In such a marvelous time as this, I feel an overwhelming debt of gratitude. I thank my Father in Heaven for blessings unnumbered and incalculable, first and foremost being the gift of His Only Begotten Son, Jesus of Nazareth, our Savior and King. I testify that Christ's perfect life and loving sacrifice constituted literally a King's ransom, an atonement willingly paid, to lead us not only from death's prison but also from the prisons of sorrow and sin and self-indulgence.

I know that Joseph Smith beheld the Father and the Son and that this day is a direct extension of that day. I owe much for the precious knowledge of which I testify here. I owe much for the priceless heritage that has been given to me. Indeed, I owe everything, and I pledge the rest of my life in giving it.

Notes

From a talk given at general conference, April 2000.

1. *Times and Seasons,* 1 May 1844, 522–23.
2. George A. Smith, in *Deseret News Weekly,* 17 July 1872, 348.
3. J. Reuben Clark Jr., in Conference Report, October 1947, 155; or Clark, "To Them of the Last Wagon," *Ensign,* July 1997, 35–36.
4. "Extracts from H. C. Kimball's Journal," *Times and Seasons,* 15 April 1845, 867; see Orson F. Whitney, *Life of Heber C. Kimball,* 2d ed. (Salt Lake City: Stevens & Wallace, 1945), 67–68.
5. See Andrew Karl Larson, *Red Hills of November: A Pioneer Biography of Utah's Cotton Town* (Salt Lake City: Deseret News Press, 1957), 311–13.
6. See *Biographies and Reminiscences from the James Henry Moyle Collection,* ed. Gene A. Sessions (Salt Lake City: The Archives of the Church of Jesus Christ of Latter-day Saints, 1974), 202–3; see also Vaughn J. Featherstone, *Man of Holiness* (Salt Lake City: Deseret Book, 1998), 140–41.

STAY THE COURSE

15

A Handful of Meal
and a Little Oil

I n response to King Ahab's great wickedness, the Lord, through the prophet Elijah, sealed the heavens, that neither dew nor rain should fall throughout all the land of Israel. The drought that ensued and the famine that followed affected Elijah himself as well as untold others in the process.

Ravens did bring Elijah bread and meat to eat, but unless ravens carry more than I think they do, this was not a gourmet meal. And ere long the brook Cherith, near which he hid and from which he drank, ran dry. And so it went for three years.

As the prophet prepared for a final confrontation with Ahab, God commanded Elijah to go to the village of Zarephath where, He said, He had commanded a widow woman to sustain him.

As he entered the city in his weary condition, he met his benefactress, who was undoubtedly as weak and wasted as he.

Perhaps almost apologetically the thirsty traveler importuned, "Fetch me, I pray thee, a little water in a vessel, that I may drink." As she turned to meet his request, Elijah added even more strain to the supplication. "Bring me, I pray thee, a morsel of bread in thine hand [also]."

Elijah's pitiful circumstances were obvious. Furthermore, the widow had been prepared by the Lord for this request. But in her own weakened and dispirited condition, the prophet's last entreaty was more than this faithful little woman could bear. In her hunger and fatigue and motherly anguish, she cried out to the stranger, "As the Lord thy God liveth, I have not a cake, but an handful of meal in a barrel, and a little oil in a cruse: and, behold, I am gathering two sticks [which tells us how small her fire needed to be], that I may go in and dress it for me and my son, that we may eat it, and die."

But Elijah was on the Lord's errand. Israel's future—including the future of this very widow and her son—was at stake. His prophetic duty made him more bold than he might normally have wanted to be.

"Fear not," he said to her, "but make me thereof a little cake first, and bring it unto me, and after make for thee and for thy son.

"For thus saith the Lord God of Israel, The barrel of meal shall not waste, neither shall the cruse of oil fail, until the day that the Lord sendeth rain upon the earth."

Then this understated expression of faith—as great, under these circumstances, as any I know in the scriptures. The record says simply, "And she went and did according to the saying of Elijah." Perhaps uncertain what the cost of her faith would be not only to herself but to her son as well, she first took her small loaf to Elijah, obviously trusting that if there were not enough bread left over, at least she and her son would have died in an act of pure charity. The story goes on, of course, to a very happy ending for her and for her son (1 Kgs. 17:10–15).

This woman is like another widow whom Christ admired so much—she who cast her farthing, her two mites, into the synagogue treasury and thereby gave more, Jesus said, than all others who had given that day (see Mark 12:41–44).

Unfortunately, the names of these two women are not recorded in the scriptures, but if I am ever so privileged in the eternities to meet them, I would like to fall at their feet and say "Thank you." Thank you for the beauty of your lives, for the wonder of your example, for the godly spirit within you prompting such "charity out of a pure heart" (1 Tim. 1:5).

Indeed, I wish to do something a little more immediate in their behalf today. I wish to speak for the widow, the fatherless, the disadvantaged and downtrodden, the hungry, the homeless, and the cold. I wish to speak for those God has always loved and spoken of in an urgent way (see D&C 58:11). I wish to speak of the poor.

There is a particularly reprehensible moment in the Book of Mormon in which a group of vain and unchristian Zoramites, after climbing atop their Rameumptom and declaring their special standing before God, immediately proceed to cast the poor from their synagogues, synagogues these needy had labored with their own hands to build. They were cast out, the record says, simply because of their poverty. In a penetrating scriptural line that forever speaks to the real plight and true pain of the impoverished, the Book of Mormon says, "They were poor as to things of the world; *and also they were poor in heart.*" Indeed, they were

145

"poor in heart, *because of their poverty as to the things of the world*" (Alma 32:3–4; emphasis added).

Directly countering the arrogance and exclusivity which the Zoramites had shown these people, Amulek gives a stirring sermon on the Atonement of Jesus Christ. Teaching that Christ's gift would be "infinite and eternal," an offering to every man, woman, and child who would ever live in this world, he also bore witness of the mercy of such a gift. He listed all the ways and all the places in which people should pray for that atoning mercy, "for your welfare," he said, "and also for the welfare of those who are around you" (Alma 34:10, 14, 27).

But this masterful discourse on the Atonement is not finished. With great directness, Amulek says of these fervent prayers: "Do not suppose that this is all; for after ye have done all these things, if ye turn away the needy, and the naked, and visit not the sick and afflicted, and impart of your substance, if ye have [it], to those who stand in need—I say unto you, if ye do not any of these things, behold, your prayer is vain, and availeth you nothing, and ye are as hypocrites who do deny the faith" (Alma 34:28). If this is the message to those who had so little, what must it mean for us?

Amulek uses here precisely the same theo-logic that King Benjamin had used fifty years earlier. After teaching the people of Zarahemla of the fall of Adam and the Atonement of Jesus Christ, Benjamin saw his congregation literally fall to the ground, viewing themselves in a state of great need, viewing themselves, he said, as less than the dust of the earth. (The difference between this response and that of the Rameumptom set goes without saying.)

"And they all cried aloud with one voice, saying: O have mercy, and apply the atoning blood of Christ that we may

146

receive forgiveness of our sins, and our hearts may be purified" (Mosiah 4:2).

With these people so teachably humble and with mercy, that loveliest of words, on every lip and tongue, King Benjamin says of the Atonement and the remission of sins:

"If God, who has created you, on whom you are dependent for your lives and for all that ye have and are, doth grant unto you whatsoever ye ask that is right, . . . O then, how ye ought to impart of the substance that ye have one to another." "Succor those that stand in need of your succor; . . . administer of your substance unto him that standeth in need." "Are we not all beggars? Do we not all depend upon the same Being, even God, for all the substance which we have?"

"For the sake of retaining a remission of your sins," King Benjamin concludes, " . . . ye should impart of your substance to the poor, every man according to that which he hath, such as feeding the hungry, clothing the naked, visiting the sick and administering to their relief, both spiritually and temporally, according to their wants" (Mosiah 4:21, 16, 19, 26).

We may not yet be the Zion of which our prophets foretold and toward which the poets and priests of Israel have pointed us, but we long for it, and we keep working toward it. I do not know whether a full implementation of such a society can be realized until Christ comes, but I know that when He did come to the Nephites, His majestic teachings and ennobling spirit led to the happiest of all times, a time in which "there were no contentions and disputations among them, and every man did deal justly one with another. And they had all things common among them; therefore there were not rich and poor, bond and free, but they were all made free, and partakers of the heavenly gift" (4 Ne. 1:2–3). That blessed circumstance was, I suppose,

147

achieved on only one other occasion of which we know—the city of Enoch, where "they were of one heart and one mind, and dwelt in righteousness; and there was no poor among them" (Moses 7:18).

The Prophet Joseph Smith had such a grand view of our possibilities, a view given him by the revelations of God. He knew that the real task was in being more Christlike—caring the way the Savior cared, loving the way He loved, "every man seeking the interest of his neighbor," the scripture says, "and doing all things with an eye single to the glory of God" (D&C 82:19).

That was what Jacob in the Book of Mormon had taught, that "after ye have obtained a hope in Christ ye shall obtain riches, if ye seek them; and ye will seek them for the intent to do good—to clothe the naked, and to feed the hungry, and to liberate the captive, and administer relief to the sick and the afflicted" (Jacob 2:19).

I pay tribute to all of you, to all who do so much and care so deeply and labor with "the intent to do good." So many are so generous. I know that some of you are struggling to make ends meet in your own lives and still you find something to share. As King Benjamin cautioned his people, it is not intended that we run faster than we have strength and all things should be done in order (see Mosiah 4:27). I love you, and your Heavenly Father loves you for all you are trying to do.

Furthermore, I know that this message is not going to cut through the centuries of temporal inequity that have plagued humankind, but I also know that the gospel of Jesus Christ holds the answer to every social and political and economic problem this world has ever faced. And I know we can each do something, however small that act may seem to be. We can pay an honest tithe and give our fast and freewill offerings, according to our circumstances. And we can watch for other ways to help. To worthy causes and needy people, we can give time if we don't have money, and we can give love when our time runs out. We can share the loaves we have and trust God that the cruse of oil will not fail.

"And thus, in their prosperous circumstances, they did not send away any who were naked, or that were hungry, or that were athirst, or that were sick, or that had not been nourished; and they did not set their hearts upon riches; therefore they were liberal to all, both old and young, both bond and free, both male and female, whether out of the church or in the church, having no respect to persons as to those who stood in need" (Alma 1:30).

How much that passage from the first chapter of Alma sounds like the wonder that was Nauvoo. Said the Prophet Joseph in that blessed time: "Respecting how much a man . . . shall give . . . we have no special instructions . . . ; he is to feed the hungry, to clothe the naked, to provide for the widow, to dry up the tear of the orphan, to comfort the afflicted, whether in this church, or in any other, or in no church at all, wherever he finds them."[1]

Remember what the Book of Mormon taught us. It is difficult enough to be poor in material goods, but the greater pain is in the heavy heart, the dwindling hope, the damaged dreams, the parental anguish, the childhood disappointment that almost always attend such circumstances.

I began with a story of diminishing cornmeal. May I conclude with another. Amidst the terrible hostilities in Missouri that would put the Prophet in Liberty Jail and see thousands of Latter-day Saints driven from their homes, Sister Drusilla

Hendricks and her invalid husband, James, who had been shot by enemies of the Church in the Battle of Crooked River, arrived with their children at a hastily shaped dugout in Quincy, Illinois, to live out the spring of that harrowing year.

Within two weeks the Hendrickses were on the verge of starvation, having only one spoonful of sugar and a saucerful of cornmeal remaining in their possession. In the great tradition of Latter-day Saint women, Drusilla made mush out of it for James and the children, thus stretching its contents as far as she could make it go. When that small offering was consumed by her famished family, she washed everything, cleaned their little dugout as thoroughly as she could, and quietly waited to die.

Not long thereafter, the sound of a wagon brought Drusilla to her feet. It was their neighbor Reuben Allred. He said he had a feeling they were out of food, so on his way into town he'd had a sack of grain ground into meal for them.

Shortly thereafter Alexander Williams arrived with two bushels of meal on his shoulder. He told Drusilla that he'd been extremely busy, but the Spirit had whispered to him that "Brother Hendricks' family is suffering, so I dropped everything and came [running]."[2]

May God, who has blessed all of us so mercifully and many of us so abundantly, bless us with one thing more. May He bless us to hear the often silent cries of the sorrowing and the afflicted, the downtrodden, the disadvantaged, the poor. Indeed, may He bless us to hear the whispering of the Holy Spirit when any neighbor anywhere "is suffering," and to "drop everything and come running," I pray in the name of the Captain of the poor, even the Lord Jesus Christ.

Notes

From a talk given at general conference, April 1996.

1. Joseph Smith, in *Times and Seasons*, 15 March 1842, 732.
2. Drusilla Doris Hendricks, in "Historical Sketch of James Hendricks and Drusilla Doris Hendricks," Historical Department, Archives Division, The Church of Jesus Christ of Latter-day Saints, Salt Lake City, typescript, 14–15.

16

To Stay and Serve
If Called Upon

In this sesquicentennial year when we are celebrating the great pioneer heritage that has come to us from the early years of this Church, it has been our good fortune to hear some of those pioneer stories which teach what the early Saints did for us and the great lessons of faith and courage they left to us. In these few pages I wish to add just one missionary footnote to what you've heard before. In doing so, I wish to speak of missions and the calls that come to the young men of the Church.

When President Brigham Young learned of the plight of those handcart companies caught in the early and devastating Wyoming winter of 1856, he called from this pulpit for teams, supplies, and provisions to be sent to the stranded Saints immediately. One in the number who responded to that call was a relatively young convert to the Church by the name of Dan Jones.

After facing a blizzard at South Pass and working their way

up the Sweetwater, these rescuers first came upon the lead group of Brother James G. Willie's company east of Rocky Ridge. "We found them in a condition that would stir the feelings of the hardest heart," Brother Jones recorded.[1] They had no fuel, they had no food, they were literally, by turns, freezing and starving to death. Burying the dead and leaving provisions for those still strong enough to use them, the rescuers moved on, fully realizing the danger the other companies were in, particularly when there was still no sign of them by the time the relief team had fought their way as far as Devil's Gate.

Brother Jones and two others were designated as a scouting team to move out to find the other companies. They did, near what would later be called Martin's Cove. Ascending a long, slushy, muddy hill, these poor travelers brought to Brother Jones's eyes a "condition of human distress," he said, "which I have never seen before or since."

Brother Edward Martin's handcart company was spread out for three or four miles. Old men were pulling and tugging their carts, sometimes loaded with a sick wife or children. Often enough it was the wife who was pulling the cart, either alongside an ill (or in place of a deceased) husband. Little children were crying and struggling through the mud and the snow. As night came, the mud froze on the children's clothing, hands, and feet, adding to the frostbite, the suffering, and, too often, the death. Charles Decker remarked that on his fifty trips across the plains (he was a mail carrier), this was the darkest hour he had ever seen in his life. Even the cattle and horses of the emigrants were dying as rapidly as the travelers.

The problem, of course, was that now the winter storms were setting in with severity, and the provisions these first riders had been able to bring amounted to almost nothing among so many people who were so near to starvation and death. The only answer was to get these pitiful groups to the safety of the Salt Lake Valley as soon as possible.

A proposal was put forward to carry only people and minimal provisions for them back to the valley, leaving every other good and possession behind at Devil's Gate, under guard until spring. When he heard the plan, Captain George D. Grant, one of the leaders of the rescue party, said, "I have thought of this, but there are no provisions to leave with them and it would be asking too much of anyone to stay here and starve [to death] for the sake of these goods; besides," he said, "where is there a man to stay [and serve] if called upon." Dan Jones spoke up and said, "Any of us would [and I will]."

Of that moment Brother Jones later wrote: "There was not money enough on earth to have hired me to stay. I had left home for only a few days and was not prepared to remain so long away; but I remembered my assertion that any of us would stay if called upon. I could not [break my word.]" As the rescue wagons pulled out to return to the valley, Brother Jones told his men that if any were worried about suffering and starvation, they were free to leave with the company. All voted to stay and take their chances.

Because of the severe winter, it would be more than five months before help and provisions would finally arrive. The little bread and salt they had quickly ran out. Hunting brought almost no success in such severe weather. Little by little they killed and ate the last of the starving cattle herd. The poorest, inedible parts they had intended to use for wolf bait, but eventually they themselves had to eat all such elements of the animals. Finally the hides themselves were consumed. As the brethren ate, they often became violently ill. Many recorded

155

that they eventually got sick just thinking of eating such distasteful material.

Brother Jones said, "We asked the Lord to bless our stomachs and adapt them to this food. We hadn't the faith to ask him to bless the cowhide." But "the brethren did not murmur," he said. "They felt to trust in God."

After four months, they had eaten every part of the cattle that could be humanly consumed and also had eaten the leather wrappings from the wagon-tongues, the soles of old moccasins, and a piece of buffalo hide that had been used for a foot mat for two months.

Now for the specific missionary point I mentioned earlier. After months of such service and deprivation, it is hard to believe that anyone—even the cruelest of men—would want to do this group harm, but apostates from the Church being what they were, I suppose it shouldn't be surprising that they planned trouble. Just as Brigham Young was preparing to send out the earliest possible help and provisions that could get through in the spring, a company of disaffected renegades started for Devil's Gate, knowing that valuable personal possessions were being stored there, the only possessions some of those handcart pioneers owned in this world. It was their intent to take the goods by force if necessary and to move on east with them as bounty.

As this group approached the fort at Devil's Gate, Brother Jones came out of the barricade alone, walking some thirty yards toward his opponents. As they started to move in, he placed his hand on his pistol and told them to halt. "I explained our situation," he said. "I told them that we were custodians of the goods that had been left there and that we did not, in fact, know whose they were." Brother Jones acknowledged there were *many* things they did not know. But he said the one thing they *did* know was that President Brigham Young had called them to this assignment, and they were determined to fulfill their responsibility. Their allegiance to God and His prophet was the only allegiance they had in this circumstance, and it was an allegiance they were determined to maintain.

As the marauders again started to make their move, Dan Jones said something like this: "We've been here all winter eating cow's gristle and rawhide, nearly freezing to death to take care of those emigrants' possessions. If you think you can take this fort after what we have given to stay here, just try it. Now I dare you to take one more step toward those goods." There was a deadly silence. No one moved. It was a breathless moment. Then the enemy leader said, "Dan Jones, I think you are [blankety blank] fool enough to die before you would give up those goods." Brother Jones said, "Thank you. I am glad you understand me so correctly."

That story then goes on to a happy ending. The enemies rode away empty-handed. Provisions came, and the guardian crew returned to their homes, seeing the protected goods returned to their rightful emigrant owners in the valley. I leave with you such a brief story of a missionary, for that is what Dan Jones was in his assignment and that is what each of you must prepare to be. When the call to serve came, he responded. When his particular assignment involved more than he had bargained for and was harder than he expected, he accepted that as well. And when enemies of the Church, malicious men, might have done him harm or otherwise damaged his faith, he said to them just one thing. "There are many things I don't know. What I do know is that a prophet of God has sent me here. I will be true to that trust placed in me."

The Aaronic Priesthood is rightly called the "preparatory

priesthood." May God bless you young men right now to pre-pare for your missions, missions which will require you to be—and prepare you to be—strong and courageous and faithful for the rest of your lives, wherever the labor or whatever the cir-cumstances. When the Lord and His leaders say, "Who will stay and serve if called upon?" say, "I will."

Notes

From a talk prepared for an Aaronic Priesthood sesquicentennial fireside, 18 May 1997.

1. The quotations from this account are from Daniel W. Jones, *Forty Years Among the Indians* (Salt Lake City: Bookcraft, 1960), 62, 66, 69, 70, 80, 104–5.

17

THE OTHER PRODIGAL

A mong the most memorable parables the Savior ever told is the story of a foolish younger brother who went to his father, asked for his portion of the estate, and left home to squander his inheritance, the scripture says, in "riotous living" (Luke 15:13). His money and his friends disappeared sooner than he thought possible—they always do—and a day of terrible reckoning came thereafter—it always does. In the downward course of all this, he became a keeper of pigs, one so hungry, so stripped of sustenance and dignity that "he would fain have filled his belly with the husks that the swine did eat" (v. 16). But even that consolation was not available to him.

Then the scripture says encouragingly, "He came to himself" (Luke 15:17). He determined to find his way home, hoping to be accepted at least as a servant in his father's household. The tender image of this boy's anxious, faithful father running to meet him and showering him with kisses is one of the most moving and compassionate scenes in all of holy writ. It tells every child of God, wayward or otherwise, how much God wants us back in the protection of His arms.

But being caught up in this younger son's story, we can miss, if we are not careful, the account of an elder son, for the opening line of the Savior's account reads, "A certain man had *two* sons" (Luke 15:11)—and He might have added, "both of whom were lost and both of whom needed to come home."

The younger son has returned, a robe has been placed on his shoulders and a ring on his finger, when the older son comes on the scene. He has been dutifully, loyally working in the field, and now he is returning. The language of parallel journeys home, though from very different locations, is central to this story.

As he approaches the house, he hears the sounds of music and laughter.

"And he called one of the servants [note that he has servants], and asked what these things meant.

"And [the servant] said unto him, Thy brother is come; and thy father hath killed the fatted calf, because he hath received him safe and sound.

"And [the older brother] was angry, and would not go in: therefore came his father out, and intreated him" (Luke 15:26–28).

You know the conversation they then had. Surely, for this father, the pain over a wayward child who had run from home and wallowed with swine is now compounded with the realization that this older, wiser brother, the younger boy's childhood hero as older brothers always are, is angry that his brother has come home.

No, I correct myself. This son is not so much angry that the other has come home as he is angry that his parents are so happy about it. Feeling unappreciated and with perhaps more than a little self-pity, this dutiful son—and he is *wonderfully dutiful*—forgets for a moment that he has never had to know filth or despair, fear or self-loathing. He forgets for a moment that every calf on the ranch is already his and so are all the robes in the closet and every ring in the drawer. He forgets for a moment that his faithfulness has been and always will be rewarded.

No, he who has virtually everything, and who has in his hardworking, wonderful way earned it, lacks the one thing that might make him the complete man of the Lord he nearly is. He has yet to come to the compassion and mercy, the charitable breadth of vision to see that *this is not a rival returning*. It is his brother. As his father pled with him to see, it is one who was dead and now is alive. It is one who was lost and now is found.

Certainly this younger brother had been a prisoner—a prisoner of sin, stupidity, and a pigsty. But the older brother lives in some confinement, too. He has, as yet, been unable to break out of the prison of himself. He is haunted by the green-eyed monster of jealousy.[1] He feels taken for granted by his father and disenfranchised by his brother, when neither is the case. He has fallen victim to a fictional affront. As such he is like Tantalus of Greek mythology—he is up to his chin in water, but he remains thirsty nevertheless. One who has heretofore presumably been very happy with his life and content with his good fortune suddenly feels very unhappy simply because another has had some good fortune as well.

Who is it that whispers so subtly in our ears that a gift given to another somehow diminishes the blessings we have received? Who makes us feel that if God is smiling on another, then He

161

surely must somehow be frowning on us? You and I both know who does this—it is "the father of all lies" (2 Ne. 2:18). It is Lucifer, our common enemy, whose cry down through the corridors of time is always and to everyone, "Give me thine honor" (Moses 4:1).

It has been said that envy is the one sin to which no one readily confesses, but just how widespread that tendency can be is suggested in the old Danish proverb, "If envy were a fever, all the world would be ill." The parson in Chaucer's *Canterbury Tales* laments it because it is so far-reaching—it can resent anything, including any virtue and talent, and it can be offended by everything, including every goodness and joy.[2] As others seem to grow larger in our sight, we think we must therefore be smaller. So, unfortunately, we occasionally act that way.

How does this happen, especially when we wish so much that it would not? I think one of the reasons is that every day we see allurements of one kind or another that tell us what we have is not enough. Someone or something is forever telling us we need to be more handsome or more wealthy, more applauded or more admired than we see ourselves as being. We are told we haven't collected enough possessions or gone to enough fun places. We are bombarded with the message that on the *world's* scale of things we have been weighed in the balance and found wanting (see Dan. 5:27; double entendre doubly intended). Some days it is as if we have been locked in a cubicle of a great and spacious building where the only thing on the TV is a never-ending soap opera entitled *Vain Imaginations* (see 1 Ne. 12:18).

But God does not work this way. The father in this story does not tantalize his children. He does not mercilessly measure them against their neighbors. He doesn't even compare them with each other. His gestures of compassion toward one do not require a withdrawal or denial of love for the other. He is divinely generous to both of these sons. Toward both of his children he extends charity. I believe God is with us the way my precious wife, Pat, is with my singing. She is a gifted musician, something of a musical genius, but I couldn't capture a musical note with Velcro. And yet I know she loves me in a very special way when I try to sing. I know that because I can see it in her eyes. They are the eyes of love.

One observer has written: "In a world that constantly compares people, ranking them as more or less intelligent, more or less attractive, more or less successful, it is not easy to really believe in a [divine] love that does not do the same. When I hear someone praised," he says, "it is hard not to think of myself as less praiseworthy; when I read about the goodness and kindness of other people, it is hard not to wonder whether I myself am as good and kind as they; and when I see trophies, rewards, and prizes being handed out to special people, I cannot avoid asking myself why that didn't happen to me."[3] If left unresisted, we can see how this inclination so embellished by the world will ultimately bring a resentful, demeaning view of God and a terribly destructive view of ourselves. Most "thou shalt not" commandments are meant to keep us from hurting others, but I am convinced the commandment not to covet is meant to keep us from hurting ourselves.

How can we overcome such a tendency so common in almost everyone? For one thing, we can do as these two sons did and start making our way back to the Father. We should do so with as much haste and humility as we can summon. Along the way we can count our many blessings, and we can applaud the accomplishments of others. Best of all, we can serve others, the finest exercise for the heart ever prescribed. But, finally, these will not be enough. When we are lost, we can "come to ourselves," but we may not always be able to "find ourselves," and, worlds without end, we cannot "save ourselves." Only the Father and His Only Begotten Son can do that. Salvation is in Them only. So we pray that They will help us, that They will "come out" to meet and embrace us and bring us into the feast They have prepared.

They will do this! The scriptures are replete with the promise that God's grace is sufficient (see Ether 12:26; Moro. 10:32; D&C 17:8). This is one arena where no one has to claw or compete. Nephi declares that the Lord "loveth the [whole] world" and has given salvation freely.

"Hath [He] commanded *any* that they should *not* partake of his goodness?" Nephi asks. No! "All . . . are privileged the one like unto the other, and none are forbidden [at His hand]."

"Come unto me all ye ends of the earth," He pleads, and buy milk without money and honey without price (see 2 Ne. 26:24–28; emphasis added). *All are privileged, the one like unto the other.* Walk peacefully. Walk confidently. Walk without fear and without envy. Be reassured of Heavenly Father's abundance to you always.

As we do this, we can help others, calling down blessings on them even as they make supplication for us. We can cheer every talent and ability, wherever it is bestowed, thus making life here more nearly what it will be like in heaven.

It will help us always to remember Paul's succinct prioritizing of virtues—"Now abideth faith, hope, charity, these three; but the greatest of these is charity" (1 Cor. 13:13). He reminds us we are *all* of the body of Christ and that *all* members, whether comely or feeble, are adored, essential, and important. We feel the depth of his plea that there "be no schism in the body, but that the members . . . have the same care one for another. And [when] one member suffer[s], all the members suffer with it; or [when] one member [is] honoured, all the members rejoice" (1 Cor. 12:25–26). That incomparable counsel helps us remember that the word *generosity* has the same derivation as the word *genealogy*, both coming from the Latin *genus,* meaning of the same birth or kind, the same family or gender.[4] We will always find it easier to be generous when we remember that this person being favored is truly one of our own.

Brothers and sisters, I testify that no one of us is less treasured or cherished of God than another. I testify that He loves each of us—insecurities, anxieties, self-image, and all. He doesn't measure our talents or our looks; He doesn't measure our professions or our possessions. He cheers on *every* runner, calling out that the race is against sin, *not* against each other. I know that if we will be faithful, there is a perfectly tailored robe of righteousness ready and waiting for *everyone* (see Isa. 61:10; 2 Ne. 4:33; 9:14), "robes . . . made . . . white in the blood of the Lamb" (Rev. 7:14).

Notes

From a talk given at general conference, April 2002.

1. See William Shakespeare, *The Merchant of Venice,* act 3, scene 2, line 110.

2. See Geoffrey Chaucer, *The Canterbury Tales,* ed. Walter W. Skeat (New York: Modern Library, 1929), 534–35.

3. Henri J. M. Nouwen, *The Return of the Prodigal Son: A Meditation on Fathers, Brothers, and Sons* (New York: Doubleday, 1992), 103.

4. I am indebted to Henri Nouwen for pointing out this etymological link.

18

"CAST NOT AWAY THEREFORE YOUR CONFIDENCE"

There is a lesson in the Prophet Joseph Smith's account of the First Vision which virtually every Latter-day Saint has had occasion to experience, or one day soon will. It is the plain and very sobering truth that before great moments, certainly before great spiritual moments, there can come adversity, opposition, and darkness. Life has some of those moments for us, and occasionally they come just as we are approaching an important decision or a significant step in our lives.

In that marvelous account which we read too seldom, Joseph said he had scarcely begun his prayer when he felt a power of astonishing influence come over him. "Thick darkness," as he described it, gathered around him and seemed bent on his utter destruction (JS–H 1:15). But he exerted all his powers to call upon God to deliver him out of the power of this enemy, and as he did so a pillar of light brighter than the noonday sun descended gradually until it rested upon him. At the very moment of the light's appearance, he found himself delivered from the destructive power which had held him bound. What then followed is the greatest epiphany since the events surrounding the Crucifixion, Resurrection, and Ascension of Christ in the meridian of time. The Father and the Son appeared to Joseph Smith, and the dispensation of the fulness of times had begun (see JS–H 1:16–17).

Most of us do not need any more reminders than we have already had that there is one who personifies "opposition in all things," that "an angel of God" fell "from heaven" and in so doing became "miserable forever." What a chilling destiny! Because this is Lucifer's fate, "he sought also the misery of all mankind," Lehi teaches us (2 Ne. 2:11, 17–18).

An entire article could be devoted to this subject of the adversary's strong, preliminary, anticipatory opposition to many of the good things God has in store for us. But I want to move past that observation to another truth we may not recognize so readily. This is a lesson in the parlance of the athletic contest that reminds us "it isn't over until it's over." It is the reminder that the fight goes on. Unfortunately we must not think Satan is defeated with that first strong breakthrough which so dramatically brought the light and moved us forward.

To make my point a little more vividly, may I go to another passage of scripture, indeed, to another vision. You will recall that the book of Moses begins with him being taken up to "an exceedingly high mountain" where, the scripture says, "he saw God face to face, and he talked with him, and the glory of God was upon Moses." What then followed was what happens to prophets who are taken to high mountains. The Lord said to Moses:

"Look, and I will show thee the workmanship of mine hands. . . . Moses looked, and . . . beheld the earth, yea, even all of it; and there was not a particle of it which he did not behold, discerning it by the spirit of God. And he beheld also the inhabitants thereof, and there was not a soul which he beheld not" (Moses 1:1–2, 4, 8, 27–28).

This experience is remarkable by every standard. It is one of the great revelations given in human history. It stands with the greatest accounts we have of any prophet's experience with Divinity.

But Moses' message to you today is: Don't let your guard down. Don't assume that a great revelation, some marvelous, illuminating moment, the opening of an inspired path, is the end of it. Remember, it isn't over until it's over.

What happens to Moses next, *after* his revelatory moment, would be ludicrous if it were not so dangerous and so true to form. Lucifer—in an effort to continue his opposition, in his unfailing effort to get his licks in later if not sooner—appears and shouts in equal portions of anger and petulance after God has revealed Himself to the prophet: "Moses, worship me." But Moses is not having it. He has just seen the real thing, and by comparison this sort of performance is pretty dismal.

"Moses looked upon Satan and said: Who art thou? . . . Where is thy glory, that I should worship thee?

"For behold, I could not look upon God, except his glory should come upon me. . . . But I can look upon thee in the natural man. . . .

". . . Where is thy glory, for it is darkness unto me? And I can judge between thee and God. . . .

"Get thee hence, Satan; deceive me not" (Moses 1:12–16).

169

The record then depicts a reaction that is both pathetic and frightening:

"And now, when Moses had said these words, Satan cried with a loud voice, and ranted upon the earth, and commanded, saying: I am the Only Begotten, worship me.

"And it came to pass that Moses began to fear exceedingly; and as he began to fear, he saw the bitterness of hell. Nevertheless, calling upon God [the very phrase used by Joseph Smith], he received strength, and he commanded, saying: Depart from me, Satan, for this one God only will I worship, which is the God of glory.

"And now Satan began to tremble, and the earth shook. . . .

"And it came to pass that Satan cried with a loud voice, with weeping, and wailing, and gnashing of teeth; and he departed hence" (Moses 1:19–22), always to come again, we can be sure, but always to be defeated by the God of glory—always.

I wish to encourage every one of us regarding the opposition that so often comes after enlightened decisions have been made, after moments of revelation and conviction have given us a peace and an assurance we thought we would never lose. In his letter to the Hebrews, the Apostle Paul was trying to encourage new members who had just joined the Church, who undoubtedly had had spiritual experiences and received the pure light of testimony, only to discover that their troubles had not ended but that some of them had just begun.

Paul pleaded with those new members in much the same way President Gordon B. Hinckley is pleading with new members today. The reminder is that we cannot sign on for a battle of such eternal significance and everlasting consequence without knowing it will be a fight—a good fight and a winning fight, but a fight nevertheless. Paul says to those who thought a new testimony, a personal conversion, a spiritual baptismal experience would put them beyond trouble—to these he says, "Call to remembrance the former days, in which, *after ye were illuminated*, ye endured a great fight of afflictions." Then this tremendous counsel, which is at the heart of my counsel to you: "*Cast not away therefore your confidence*, which hath great recompence of reward.

"For ye have need of patience, that, after ye have done the will of God, ye might receive the promise.

" . . . If any man draw back, my soul shall have no pleasure in him.

" . . . We are not of them who draw back unto perdition" (Heb. 10:32, 35–36, 38–39; emphasis added).

In Latter-day Saint talk that is to say, Sure it is tough—before you join the Church, while you are trying to join, and after you have joined. That is the way it has always been, Paul says, but don't draw back. Don't panic and retreat. Don't lose your confidence. Don't forget how you once felt. Don't distrust the experience you had. That tenacity is what saved Moses and Joseph Smith when the adversary confronted them, and it is what will save you.

I suppose every returned missionary and probably every convert reading these words knows exactly what I am talking about. Appointments for discussions canceled, the Book of Mormon in a plastic bag hanging from a front doorknob, baptismal dates not met. And so it goes through the teaching period, through the commitments and the baptism, through the first weeks and months in the Church, and more or less forever—at least, the adversary would pursue it forever if he thought he could see any weakening of your resolve, any chink in your armor.

This opposition turns up almost any place something good

has happened. It can happen when you are trying to get an education. It can hit you after your first month in your new mission field. It certainly happens in matters of love and marriage. It can occur in situations related to your family, Church callings, or career.

With any major decision there are cautions and considerations to make, but once there has been illumination, beware the temptation to retreat from a good thing. If it was right when you prayed about it and trusted it and lived for it, it is right now. Don't give up when the pressure mounts. Certainly don't give in to that being who is bent on the destruction of your happiness. Face your doubts. Master your fears. "Cast not away therefore your confidence." Stay the course and see the beauty of life unfold for you.

To help us make our way through these experiences, these important junctures in our lives, let me draw from another scriptural reference to Moses. It was given in the early days of this dispensation when revelation was needed, when a true course was being set and had to be continued.

Most Latter-day Saints know the formula for revelation given in section 9 of the Doctrine and Covenants—the verses about studying it out in your mind and the Lord promising to confirm or deny. What most of us don't read in conjunction with this is the section which precedes it: section 8.

In that revelation the Lord has said, "I will tell you in your mind and in your heart, by the Holy Ghost, which shall come upon you and which shall dwell in your heart." I love the combination there of both mind and heart. God will teach us in a reasonable way and in a revelatory way—mind and heart combined—by the Holy Ghost. "Now, behold," He continues, "*this is the spirit of revelation; behold, this is the spirit by which*

172

Moses brought the children of Israel through the Red Sea on dry ground" (D&C 8:2–3; emphasis added).

Why would the Lord use the example of crossing the Red Sea as the classic example of "the spirit of revelation"? Why didn't He use the First Vision? Or the example from the book of Moses we just used? Or the vision of the brother of Jared? Well, He could have used any of these, but He didn't. Here He had another purpose in mind.

Usually we think of revelation as a downpour of information. But this is too narrow a concept of revelation. May I suggest how section 8 broadens our understanding, particularly in light of these "fights of affliction" we have been discussing.

First of all, revelation almost always comes in response to a question, usually an urgent question—not always, but usually. In that sense it does provide information, but it is urgently needed information, special information. Moses' challenge was how to get himself and the children of Israel out of this horrible predicament they were in. There were chariots behind them, sand dunes on every side, and a lot of water immediately ahead. He needed information to know what to do, but it wasn't a casual thing he was asking. In this case it was literally a matter of life and death.

You will need information too, but in matters of great consequence it is not likely to come unless you want it urgently, faithfully, humbly. Moroni calls it seeking "with real intent" (Moro. 10:4). If you can seek that way and stay in that mode, not much that the adversary can counter with will dissuade you from a righteous path. You can hang on, whatever the assault and affliction, because you have paid the price for real conviction.

Like Moses in that vision, there may come after the fact some competing doubts and confusion, but these will pale when you measure them against the real thing. *Remember the real thing.* Remember how urgently you have needed help in earlier times and you got it. The Red Sea will open to the honest seeker of revelation. The adversary has power to hedge up the way, to marshal Pharaoh's forces and dog our escape right to the water's edge, but he can't produce the real thing. He cannot conquer if we will it otherwise. Exerting all our powers, the light will again come, the darkness will again retreat, the safety will be sure. That is lesson number one about crossing the Red Sea by the spirit of revelation.

Lesson number two is closely related. It is that in the process of revelation and making important decisions, fear plays a destructive, sometimes paralyzing role. To Oliver Cowdery, who missed the opportunity of a lifetime because he didn't seize it in the lifetime of the opportunity, the Lord said, "You did not continue as you commenced." Does that sound familiar to those who have been illuminated and then knuck-led under to second thoughts and returning doubts? "It is not expedient that you should translate now," the Lord said in language that must have been very hard for Oliver to hear. "Behold, it was expedient when you commenced; *but you feared,* and the time is past, and it is not expedient now" (D&C 9:5, 10–11; emphasis added).

Everyone runs the risk of fear. For a moment in Moses' confrontation with the adversary, "Moses began to fear exceedingly; and as he began to fear, he saw the bitterness of hell" (Moses 1:20). That's when you see it—when you are afraid.

That is exactly the problem that beset the children of Israel at the edge of the Red Sea, and it has everything to do with holding fast to your earlier illumination. The record says, "And when Pharaoh drew nigh, the children of Israel lifted up their eyes, and, behold, the Egyptians marched after them; and they were sore afraid." Some (just like those Paul described earlier) said words to this effect: "Let's go back. This isn't worth it. We must have been wrong. That probably wasn't the right spirit telling us to leave Egypt." What they actually said to Moses was: "Wherefore hast thou dealt thus with us, to carry us forth out of Egypt? . . . It had been better for us to serve the Egyptians, than that we should die in the wilderness" (Ex. 14:10–12). And I have to say, "What about that which has already happened? What about the miracles that got you here? What about the frogs and the lice? What about the rod and the serpent, the river and the blood? What about the hail, the locusts, the fire, the firstborn sons?"

How soon we forget. It would *not* have been better to stay and serve the Egyptians, and it is *not* better to remain outside the Church, nor to put off marriage, nor to reject a mission call or other Church service, and so on and so on forever. Of course, our faith will be tested as we fight through these self-doubts and second thoughts. Some days we will be miraculously led out of Egypt—seemingly free, seemingly on our way—only to come to yet another confrontation, like all that water lying before us. At those times we must resist the temptation to panic and give up. At those times fear will be the strongest of the adversary's weapons against us.

"And Moses said unto the people, *Fear ye not*, stand still, and see the salvation of the Lord. . . . The Lord shall fight for you." In confirmation the great Jehovah said to Moses, "Speak unto the children of Israel, that they go forward" (Ex. 14:13–15; emphasis added).

That is the second lesson of the spirit of revelation. After you have gotten the message, after you have paid the price to feel His love and hear the word of the Lord, go forward. Don't fear, don't vacillate, don't quibble, don't whine. You may, like Alma going to Ammonihah, have to find a route that leads an unusual way, but that is exactly what the Lord is doing here for the children of Israel. Nobody had ever crossed the Red Sea this way, but so what? There's always a first time. With the spirit of revelation, dismiss your fears and wade in with both feet. In the words of Joseph Smith, "Brethren [and sisters], shall we not go on in so great a cause? Go forward and not backward. Courage, brethren; and on, on to the victory!" (D&C 128:22).

The third lesson from the Lord's spirit of revelation in the miracle of crossing the Red Sea is that along with the illuminating revelation that points us toward a righteous purpose or duty, God will also provide the means and power to achieve that purpose. Trust in that eternal truth. If God has told you something is right, if something is indeed true for you, He will provide the way for you to accomplish it. That is true of joining the Church or raising a family, of going on a mission, or any one of a hundred other worthy tasks in life. Remember what the Savior said to the Prophet Joseph Smith in the Sacred Grove. What was the problem in 1820? Why was Joseph not to join another church? It was at least in part because "they teach for doctrines the commandments of men, having a form of godliness, but they deny the power thereof" (JS–H 1:19). God's grace is sufficient! The Lord would tell Joseph again and again that just as in days of old the children of Israel would "be led out of bondage by power, and with a stretched-out arm. . . . Therefore, let not your hearts faint. . . . Mine angels shall go up before you, and also my presence, and in time ye shall possess the goodly land" (D&C 103:17, 19–20).

What goodly land? Well, your goodly land. Your promised

land. Your new Jerusalem. Your own little acre flowing with milk and honey. Your future. Your dreams. Your destiny. I believe that in our own individual ways, God takes us to the grove or the mountain or the temple and there shows us the wonder of what His plan is for us. We may not see it as fully as Moses or Nephi or the brother of Jared did, but we see as much as we need to see in order to know the Lord's will for us and to know that He loves us beyond mortal comprehension. I also believe that the adversary and his pinched, calculating little minions try to oppose such experiences and then try to darken them after they happen. But that is not the way of the gospel. That is not the way of a Latter-day Saint who claims as the fundamental fact of the Restoration the spirit of revelation. Fighting through darkness and despair and pleading for the light is what opened this dispensation. It is what keeps it going, and it is what will keep you going. With Paul, I say to all of you:

"Cast not away therefore your confidence, which hath great recompence of reward.

"For ye have need of patience, that, after ye have done the will of God, ye might receive the promise" (Heb. 10:35–36).

I acknowledge the reality of opposition and adversity, but I bear witness of the God of glory, of the redeeming Son of God, of light and hope and a bright future. I promise you that God lives and loves you, each one of you, and that He has set bounds and limits to the opposing powers of darkness. I testify that Jesus is the Christ, the victor over death and hell and the fallen one who schemes there. The gospel of Jesus Christ is true, and it has been restored.

"Fear ye not." And when the second and third and fourth

blows come, "Fear ye not. . . . The Lord shall fight for you" (Ex. 14:13–14). "Cast not away therefore your confidence."

Note

From a devotional address given at Brigham Young University, 2 March 1999.

INDEX

Muscular dystrophy, Avila sisters
attend temple despite, 103–5
Music: in sacrament meeting, 20;
unwholesome, 25–26

Nauvoo, charity practiced in, 149
Neilson, Peter, as example of
generosity, 136–37
Nephi: testimony of, 53–54; on
salvation, 66
Nephites, righteousness of, after
Savior's visit, 147
New Testament, teachings of, 29,
33–38. See also Apostles; Jesus
Christ
Nourishment, spiritual, 9

Obedience, 26, 46, 86; and remission
of sins, 19; as prerequisite to
inspiration, 40; fostering, in
students, 41–42; necessary for
salvation, 57; and God's will, 120;
blessings a result of, 134
Offenses: endured by Savior, 94;
forgiving, 87
Opposition: purposes of, 88; spiritual
experiences accompanied by, 167,
170
Optimism, 94

Packer, Boyd K., teaching methods of,
32
Parenting: rewards of, 7–8; challenges
of, 92; example of prodigal's father,
159–60
Parents: single, 92; supporting
missionaries, 102, 109–10; sacrifices
made by, 110–11; youth to seek
counsel from, 122, 125–26
Passover, symbolism of, 17–18
Patience, 86, 171; God's, 6
Paul: on Atonement, 46; on adversity,
66–67; on cleanliness, 121; on
charity, 164–65; counsel of, to new
members of Church, 170–71
Peace: inner, 7–8, 23, 66–68; gospel as

source of, 12, 83, 88–89; search for,
84; achieving, 86, 87; in God, 95
Pentecost, day of, 36
Perfection, working toward, 41–42
Perspective, 95–97
Peter, leadership qualities of, 35–38
Pioneers, handcart, 153–57
Plan of salvation, 17, 46; role of
forgiveness in, 14
Poor: caring for the, 145; in heart,
145–46
Poverty, 145–46; consequences of, 149
Power: of gospel, 26–27; of scriptures,
27; of Holy Ghost, 51–52; of
priesthood, 118–20; of God, 176
Pratt, Parley P., mission served by, 109
Prayer: answers to, 23, 43, 93, 118–20,
136–37; fervent, 85; for guidance in
financial crisis, 130; of rescuers of
handcart companies, 156; for
mercy, 164; for others' welfare, 164;
of Joseph Smith, for deliverance,
167–68; for personal revelation,
172–74
Premortal life, 5, 21–22; gospel taught
in, 50–51
Preparedness, personal, 117–24
President of the Church, succession to
office of, 34
Priesthood: role of, 15; responsibilities
of, 111–13; worthiness to hold, 117;
power of, 118–20; bearers, as
instruments in hands of God, 120;
bearers, to flee from lust, 121;
honoring, 123–24
Priesthood, Aaronic, 117; duties of,
20–21; significance of, 125; as
preparatory priesthood, 157–58
Priesthood, Melchizedek, 117
Priorities, 11, 13, 63–64
Problems: world's solutions to, 4;
financial, faced by missionary's
family, 129–32; gospel as answer to,
148; social, political, and economic,
148
Prodigal son, parable of, 159–63
Progression, eternal, 66